BERTOLT BRECHT

The Resistible Rise of Arturo Ui

translated by
RALPH MANHEIM

with commentary and notes by
NON WORRALL

METHUEN DRAMA

Methuen Drama Student Edition

10 9 8 7

This edition first published in the United Kingdom in 2002 by
Methuen Publishing Ltd
Reprinted in 2006 by Methuen Drama
A & C Black Publishers Limited
38 Soho Square
London WID 3HB

This translation of *The Resistible Rise of Arturo Ui* first published in 1981
by Eyre Methuen Ltd by arrangement with Suhrkamp Verlag, Frankfurt am Main
Translation copyright for the play and texts by Brecht © 1981 by Stefan S. Brecht
Original work entitled *Der aufhaltsame Aufstieg des Arturo Ui*
Copyright © 1957 by Suhrkamp Verlag, Frankfurt am Main

Commentary and notes copyright © 2002 by Non Worrall

A CIP catalogue record for this book is available from the British Library

ISBN 978-0-413-77263-3

Quotation from Michael Billington: *The Modern Actor* (London: Hamish Hamilton,
1973), copyright © Michael Billington, 1973, by kind permission of Penguin Books
Ltd; quotations from Brecht: *Poems 1913–1956* (ed. John Willett and Ralph
Manheim), *Letters 1913–1956* (trans. Ralph Manheim, ed. John Willett), *Brecht on
Art and Politics* (ed. Tom Kuhn and Steven Giles), *Brecht on Theatre* (trans. and
ed. John Willett), John Willett: *Brecht in Context* by permission of Methuen
Publishing Ltd

Cover photograph: Antony Sher as Arturo Ui in the 1991 production at the Royal
National Theatre. Photograph © Clive Barda

Typeset by Deltatype Ltd, Birkenhead, Wirral
Printed and bound in Great Britain by Cox & Wyman Ltd, Reading, Berkshire

CAUTION

Contents

Bertolt Brecht: 1898–1956

Brecht's life falls into three distinct phases:

From 1898 to 1933 he is in Germany.
From 1933 to 1947 during the Hitler years, he is in forced exile from Germany in various parts of the world.
In 1947 he returns to Europe, first of all to Switzerland and then to East Berlin in the German Democratic Republic.

Germany

1898 Eugen Berthold Friedrich Brecht born on 10 February at Augsburg. Father employee, later director, of the Haindl paper mill.

1908 Goes to Augsburg Grammar School. Caspar Neher (later his designer) is one of his closest friends.

1913 Begins to contribute poems and essays to student newspaper.

1914 Begins to write poems, stories, reviews and essays for the literary supplement of local newspaper.

1915 Caspar Neher volunteers for military service. Brecht writes to him regularly.

1916 Almost expelled for unpatriotic essay on the title: 'It is a sweet and honourable thing to die for one's country'.

1917 Enrols as medical student at Munich University. Also attends Arthur Kutscher's theatre seminar. Samples bohemian literary life of the city.

1918 Conscripted into the army and serves as a medical orderly at Augsburg Military Hospital. Writes *Baal* and does theatre reviews for local newspaper. Becomes more involved in socialist political organisations.

1919 Writes *Drums in the Night*. Meets the comedian Karl Valentin, the theatre director Erich Engel and actresses Elisabeth Bergner, Blandine Ebinger, Carola Neher and Marianne Zoff. Brecht and Neher work to establish as many artistic and literary contacts as possible.

1920 Visits Berlin. His mother dies; he writes 'Song of my mother'.

1921 Brecht and Neher in financial difficulties. Preoccupied, Brecht fails to register for university course and is dropped from the university roll. Ends up in hospital suffering from malnutrition. New friendship with Arnolt Bronnen, a playwright, leads him to change the spelling of his name to Bertolt or Bert.

1922 Brecht summarises his life so far in a letter to Herbert Ihering on October 17:

> I first saw the light of the world in 1898. My parents hail from the Black Forest. Elementary school bored me for four years. In the nine years of my pickling at the Augsburg Realgymnasium I made no great contribution to my teachers' advancement. They never wearied of pointing out my penchant for idleness and independence. At the university I read medicine and learned to play the guitar. At secondary school I went in for all kinds of sports and developed a heart condition, which familiarised me with the secrets of metaphysics. During the war, I served as an orderly in a military hospital. After that I wrote a few plays, and in the spring of this year I was taken to the Charité hospital because of undernourishment. Arnolt Bronnen was unable to help me substantially out of his earnings as a sales clerk. After twenty-four years in the light of the world I have grown rather thin.
>
> (*Letters 1913–1956*, p. 71)

Marries Marianne Zoff in Munich. Writes *In the Jungle of the Cities*. First performance of *Drums in the Night* at the Deutsches Theater, Berlin.

1923 Daughter, Hanne, is born. The activities of Hitler's National

Socialists are hotly discussed in Brecht's Munich circle. First productions of *In the Jungle of the Cities* and *Baal* take place in Munich and Leipzig respectively. Meets Helene Weigel, the actress, for the first time.

1924 Directs Marlowe's *Edward II* which he and Lion Feuchtwanger – celebrated novelist and playwright as well as being dramatic adviser to the Kammerspiele in Munich – had adapted. Brecht was already using certain devices (plot summaries before scenes, white face make-up to indicate fear) to induce critical detachment in actors and audience. Finally settles in Berlin. Is taken on as dramaturg (literary adviser) at Max Reinhardt's Deutsches Theater. Helene Weigel bears him a son, Stefan. Meets Elisabeth Hauptmann who becomes his constant collaborator.

1925 Writes poems, visits Marianne Zoff and Hanne. Congratulates G.B. Shaw on his seventieth birthday, commending his 'keen intelligence and fearless eloquence'. Completes manuscript of *Man equals Man* which he presents to Elisabeth Hauptmann as thanks for her unstinting and unpaid work. Joins 'Group 25', aiming to co-ordinate the interests of younger authors not represented by literary groups dominated by the older generation.

1926 *Man equals Man* premiered at Darmstadt and Düsseldorf. Works on a play (never finished) called *Joe Fleischhacker*, which was to deal with the Chicago Wheat Exchange; leads him to the study of Marx as the only adequate method of analysing the workings of capitalism.

1927 Divorces Marianne Zoff. Works with Erwin Piscator, the pioneer of communist political theatre in Germany, on a dramatisation of Hašek's novel, *The Good Soldier Schweik*.

1928 *The Threepenny Opera*, music by Kurt Weill, words by Brecht (based on a translation of John Gay's *Beggar's Opera* by Elisabeth Hauptmann), opens at Theater am Schiffbauerdamm –

hit of the season. Brecht had transferred bourgeois manners to a Soho criminal setting.

1929 Marries Helene Weigel. *The Baden-Baden Cantata* staged at Baden-Baden Music Festival, music by Hindemith.

1930 Daughter Barbara born. His *Lehrstück* or didactic play, *The Measures Taken*, is given its first performance in Berlin. The communist didactic plays for amateur performance were intended to clarify the ideas of the performers as much as the audience. The first performance of *The Rise and Fall of the City of Mahagonny*, an opera with words by Brecht and music by Kurt Weill, causes a riot as the Nazis voice their criticism at Leipzig. In his notes on the opera, Brecht lists the differences between the traditional *dramatic* (or Aristotelian) and the new *epic* (or non-Aristotelian) theatre at which he is aiming.

1931 Completes *St Joan of the Stockyards* – not performed until 1959.

1932 Brecht's only film *Kuhle Wampe* held up by the censor. His dramatisation of Maxim Gorky's novel *The Mother* is performed by left-wing collective in Berlin, music by Hanns Eisler, and demonstrates development of a worker's mother towards proletarian class-consciousness. Beginning of friendship with Margarete Steffin. Studies Marxism under dissident communist Karl Korsch.

Exile

1933 Nazis come to power. The night after the German parliament building (the Reichstag) is burnt down, Brecht flees with his family to Prague. Moves to Vienna, then Zurich, finally settling on the island of Fyn in Denmark. Friendship with Ruth Berlau begins.

1934 Writes *The Threepenny Novel*. Redrafts, with Hanns Eisler and Margarete Steffin, *Round Heads and Pointed Heads or Empires of a Feather Flock Together. An atrocity fairy tale*. Walter

Benjamin stays with Brecht. Visits London. Themes of flight and exile enter his poems. Helene Weigel and children in Vienna and Zurich.

1935 Visits Moscow, talks to Soviet dramatist Sergei Tretiakov about the 'alienation effect'. Attends International Writers' Conference in Paris. Brecht is stripped of his German citizenship by the Nazis. Visits New York to look in on a production of *The Mother* which does not meet with his approval. Negotiates American edition of *The Threepenny Novel* and a performance of *Round Heads*.

1936 Attends International Writers' Conference in London. Lives in Hampstead. Writes anti-fascist poetry. Consultant on first production of *Round Heads* in Danish in the Riddersalen in Copenhagen.

1937 Completes the Spanish play *Señora Carrar's Rifles*. Writes children's songs for Helene Weigel. Attends International Writers' Conference in Paris: main theme, intellectuals' attitudes towards the Spanish Civil War. Brands self 'one of the cowards' for being too cautious to go to Madrid himself. First performance of *The Threepenny Opera* and *Señora Carrar's Rifles* (with Helene Weigel, 'dedicated to the heroic fight for freedom of the Spanish people') in Paris. Calls Helene Weigel's acting 'the best and the purest that could be seen so far in the epic theatre anywhere'.

1938 Franco's right-wing Falangists emerge as the likely victors in the Spanish Civil War and Chamberlain signs away the Sudetenland in the Munich Treaty in an effort to appease Hitler. The growing power of fascism, developments in the Soviet Union, his steadily diminishing chances of seeing his plays performed anywhere and the ensuing money worries increase his sense of isolation. On Easter Sunday writes the poem 'Spring 1938':

> In the willows by the sound
> These spring nights the screech-owl often calls.

> According to a peasant superstition
> Your screech-owl informs people that
> They haven't long to live. I
> Who know full well that I told the truth
> About the powers that be, don't need a death-bird
> To inform me so.
>
> (trans. Derek Bowman, *Poems 1913–1956*, Methuen, p. 304)

Fear and Misery in the Third Reich premiered in Paris. Writes *Life of Galileo*, assisted by Margarete Steffin. In December, news of fission of uranium by physicists Hahn and Strassmann causes revisions to text.

1939   Hitler annexes Czechoslovakia. Works by Brecht confiscated and pulped. Moves to Stockholm with his family. Finishes *Mother Courage and her Children*. Not allowed to participate in political activities but continues under pseudonym of John Kent. Father dies and is buried in Augsburg. Works on *The Good Person of Szechwan*. Soviet Union invades Finland.

1940   German forces march into Denmark and Norway. Moves with family to Helsinki, expressing gratitude for help and friendship he found in Stockholm:

> It's a big thing to find so much intellectual solidarity even (and especially) in these dark times . . . I had the feeling that I was leaving my home.
>
> (Letter to Henry Peter Matthis, *Letters 1913–1956*, p. 323)

Drafts *Mr Puntila and his Man Matti*, works with Hella Wuolijoki. Severe food shortage. Waits for visas to go to America.

1941   Completes *The Good Person of Szechwan*, *Mr Puntila and his Man Matti* and *The Resistible Rise of Arturo Ui*, the last in collaboration with Margarete Steffin. Writes war poetry and 'Finnish Epigrams'. Travels through the Soviet Union via Leningrad and Moscow to Vladivostock and sails to the USA. Greatly affected by death of Margarete Steffin from pneumonia in a Moscow hospital:

> In Year Nine of the flight from Hitler
> Exhausted by travelling
> By cold and by hunger in wintry Finland
> And by waiting for a passport to another continent
> Our comrade Steffin died
> In the red city of Moscow.
>> ('After the death of my collaborator M.S.', trans. John Willett,
>> *Poems 1913–1956*, p. 364)

Arrives in Los Angeles in July, settles in Santa Monica. Makes contact with other European exiles, e.g. Heinrich Mann, Lion Feuchtwanger and Fritz Lang, and also with Americans such as Orson Welles. First performance of *Mother Courage and her Children* in neutral Switzerland.

1942 Prepares *Poems in Exile* for publication. Participates in anti-war, anti-fascist activities of exile groups. Meets Charles Laughton. Finds it difficult to adjust to American values: 'but all that stands there as if it were in a showcase, and I involuntarily search every mountain and every lemon tree for a small price tag.' Registered as both subject to military service and as an 'enemy alien'.

1943 First performances of *The Good Person of Szechwan* and *Life of Galileo* in Zurich. Mussolini resigns. Brecht caught in extended argument with Thomas Mann about the differences between Germany and Hitler.

1944 Brecht becomes member of newly formed Council for a Democratic Germany. Finishes first version of *The Caucasian Chalk Circle*. Studies Arthur Waley's translations of Chinese poetry. Begins to revise *Galileo* with Charles Laughton.

1945 *Fear and Misery in the Third Reich* performed in New York under title of *The Private Life of the Master Race*. English version of *Galileo* further revised after dropping of atomic bombs on Hiroshima and Nagasaki, to stress the social responsibility of the scientist.

1946 First performance of Brecht's adaptation of Webster's *The Duchess of Malfi* in Boston.

1947 Charles Laughton appears in the title role of *Galileo* in Beverly Hills and New York. Brecht appears before the 'House Committee on Un-American Activities', proves himself master of ambiguity when cross-examined about his communist sympathies.

Return

Brecht and Helene Weigel go to Zurich, leaving son, Stefan, an American citizen, in USA. Meets up again with Caspar Neher as well as playwrights, Max Frisch and Carl Zuckmayer. First applies for Austrian passport (Weigel is Austrian).

1948 Adaptation of Sophocles' *Antigone* performed in Chur, Switzerland. *Mr Puntila and his Man Matti* premiered in Zurich. Publishes *Little Organum for the Theatre*. Travels to Berlin, starts rehearsals for *Mother Courage* at Deutsches Theater in Soviet sector of city. *The Caucasian Chalk Circle* first performed in Eric and Maja Bentley's English translation by students at Northfield, Minnesota.

1949 *Mother Courage* opens at Deutsches Theater with Helene Weigel in title role. Brecht visits Zurich again before settling in Berlin. The Berliner Ensemble, Brecht and Weigel's own state-subsidised company, is formed and opens with *Puntila*. Brecht applies again for Austrian passport.

1951 *The Mother* is performed by the Berliner Ensemble. Brecht finishes first version of adaptation of Shakespeare's *Coriolanus*.

1953 When Stalin dies in April, Brecht writes:

> The oppressed people of five continents, those who have already liberated themselves, and all those who are fighting for world peace, must have felt their hearts miss a beat when they heard that Stalin was dead. He was the embodiment of their hopes. But the intellectual

and material weapons which he produced remain, and with them the method to produce new ones.

(*Brecht on Art and Politics*, Methuen, 2002)

Brecht elected President of the German section of the PEN Club, the international writers' association. On 17 June there are strikes and demonstrations protesting about working conditions in the German Democratic Republic. Brecht angry that a doctored version of a letter he wrote is published, making it seem that he sympathised with the forcible suppression of the workers' uprising.

1954 Berliner Ensemble acquires its own home at Theater am Schiffbauerdamm. German premiere of *The Caucasian Chalk Circle* but 'The Struggle for the Valley' is omitted as being politically inopportune. Brecht makes public his objections to the Paris Treaty (which incorporated the Federal Republic of Germany into Nato) and to re-armament in general. Brecht in Bruges, Amsterdam and Paris where Berliner Ensemble gives performances of *Mother Courage* and Kleist's *The Broken Pitcher*. Productions greeted with great acclaim at the Paris Thèâtre des Nations festival. Brecht awarded Stalin Peace Prize.

1955 Travels to Moscow to receive Stalin Peace Prize. In his acceptance speech he explains how his thinking has been shaped by particular writings and events:

> The most important lesson was that a future for mankind was becoming visible only 'from below', from the standpoint of the oppressed and exploited. Only by fighting with them does one fight for mankind.
>
> (*Brecht on Art and Politics*)

By the end of the year suffering from exhaustion and unwell.

1956 Brecht's health prevents him from carrying on rehearsing, preparing Berliner Ensemble, now recognised as foremost progressive theatre in Europe, for a visit to London. Hands over

direction to Erich Engel. 14 August Brecht dies of a heart attack.
Berliner Ensemble visit to London goes ahead very successfully.
At the official memorial celebration of Brecht's life, his own
version of his epitaph is quoted:

> I need no gravestone, but
> If you need one for me
> I would like it to bear these words:
> He made suggestions. We
> Carried them out.
> Such an inscription would
> Honour us all.

> (trans. Michael Hamburger, *Poems 1913–1956*, p. 218)

Plot

This is the story of a gangster who holds the entire vegetable trade in two cities up to ransom. His name is Arturo Ui. His rise to power begins in the town of Chicago during a slump.

The small greengrocers' market has shrunk to nothing, and the members of the Cauliflower Trust, who regulate the business, are in a bad way. Arturo Ui and his gangsters have also been hit by the slump and the gang's morale is very low. To Ui, the only hope seems to lie in the gangsters taking control of the Trust. He sees the chance of breaking out of the life of a small-time hoodlum and rising to better things.

Prologue
The Announcer outlines what the play will be about and introduces the characters.

Scene 1a. Financial district of Chicago
The members of the Cauliflower Trust agree that crisis is upon them. Every day, reports of bankruptcies pour in. Arturo Ui has been waiting in their outer office for days to offer his services: he will *force* the small tradesmen to buy the surplus cauliflowers. The Trust rejects the gangster's offer. Flake, a member of the Trust, suggests that they overcome their difficulties by getting a loan from the council. This loan, officially allocated for the construction of a new quay in the shipyard, could be diverted to the Trust and thus keep them in business. The other members of the Trust express doubts that

Dogsborough, who represents the waterfront, a man well-known for his honesty, would support this chicanery. Butcher has a plan. The plan is now shown in action.

At the end of each scene a 'sign' or projected text appears which describes the parallel historical events in Germany (listed in the Chronological Table on p. 101).

Sign 1: 1929–1932. Germany is hard hit by the world crisis. At the height of the crisis a number of Prussian Junkers (landowners) try to obtain government loans, for a long time without success. The big industrialists in the Ruhr dream of expansion.

Scene 1b. Outside the produce exchange
Flake persuades Sheet to sell his shipyard to the Trust for next to nothing.

Scene 2. A back room in Dogsborough's restaurant
Members of the Trust visit Dogsborough and offer him the chance of buying the major share in Sheet's shipyard for a knockdown price as a token of the Trust's esteem for his integrity in the face of their 'stupid' request for a loan from the council. Dogsborough succumbs to the temptation when he is assured that there are no strings attached.

Sign 2: By way of winning President Hindenburg's sympathy for their cause, the Junkers make him a present of a landed estate.

Scene 3. Bookmaker's office on 122nd Street
Ui is depressed and the gang's morale is low. The Trust, having received the loan through Dogsborough's help, has surmounted the crisis. Ui's lieutenant, Roma, suggests they start a protection racket. Ui refuses to do so until he has a judge in his pocket. A newspaperman,

Ragg, enters and mocks Ui as a has-been. He is threatened and exits hurriedly. The gangster Giri enters with Bowl, who for many years has been Sheet's accountant. Bowl has been summarily sacked. He reveals the secret machinations between Dogsborough and the Trust. Ui realises that this is his chance to get into really big business.

Sign 3: In the autumn of 1932, Adolf Hitler's party and private army are threatened with bankruptcy and disintegration. To save the situation Hitler tries desperately to have himself appointed Chancellor, but for a long time Hindenburg refuses to see him.

Scene 4. Dogsborough's country house

Dogsborough regrets having accepted the gift of this country estate and the misuse of the loan. He fears an investigation. Ui and his accomplices force their way in. Ui wants Dogsborough's backing – a good word with the police and a protection deal with the Trust. He tries to blackmail the old man with his knowledge of the facts. Dogsborough refuses. The gangsters threaten to crush him. Two councillors enter and confirm that there will be an investigation but express their faith in Dogsborough's integrity.

Sign 4: In January 1933 Hindenburg appoints Hitler Chancellor in return for a promise to prevent the exposure of the *Osthilfe* (East Aid) scandal, in which Hindenburg himself is implicated.

Scene 5. City Hall

The inquiry is under way concerning the whereabouts of the missing loan and the construction of the quay. Special editions bring the news of Sheet's murder. Ui now appears representing Dogsborough and reports on his findings, which place the whole guilt of the council loan embezzlement on the deceased Sheet. To prove that Dogsborough is secretly the real owner of the shipyards, the lawyer O'Casey calls

Bowl as a witness. At a signal from one of Ui's bodyguards, Bowl is shot outside the door.

Sign 5: After coming to power legally, Hitler surprises his high patrons by extremely violent measures, but keeps his promises.

Scene 6. Hotel Mammoth. Ui's suite

To improve his image, Ui takes lessons in speechmaking, movement and posture from a classical actor.

Sign 6: The gang leader quickly transforms himself into a statesman. He is believed to have taken lessons in declamation and bearing from one Basil, a provincial actor.

Scene 7. Offices of the Cauliflower Trust

In a grandiloquent speech, with the backing of Dogsborough and Clark, Ui asks the small greengrocers for voluntary contributions – ostensibly for the maintenance of law and order by the gangsters. The tradesmen are unconvinced. Roma quietly suggests to Ui that the warehouse of Hook, one of the objectors, should be burnt to the ground to make clear to them the advisability of the contributions. Before this actually takes place, the gangsters bring in the supposed widow of the murdered Bowl and take up a 'collection' for her.

Sign 7: February 1933, the Reichstag fire. Hitler accuses his enemies of instigating the fire and gives the signal for the Night of the Long Knives.

Scene 8. The warehouse fire trial

8a

Fish, an unemployed worker, is accused of starting the fire. He appears to have been drugged. Giri, a gangster, gives evidence against him, showing no respect for the court or truth.

8b

Hook, the owner of the warehouse, tries to give evidence against the gangsters. He is threatened by them.

8c

Hook, now with a heavily bandaged head, retracts his evidence.

8d

Fish is identified as the arsonist by Dockdaisy, the woman who pretended to be the widow of Bowl. She links him with Bowl's death.

8e

Givola, a gangster, makes fun of the evidence that gasoline cans were carried out of the Cauliflower Trust offices by members of Ui's gang.

8f

Fish starts to recover and is drugged again. The judge is threatened by Giri and the trial continues.

8g

Fish is found guilty and sentenced to fifteen years' hard labour.

Sign 8: The Supreme Court in Leipzig condemns an unemployed worker to death for causing the fire. The real incendiaries get off scot-free.

Scene 9a. A street in Cicero
A woman climbs out of a shot-up truck and staggers forward. She accuses Ui of the attack and of murdering her husband. She is ignored by those she is appealing to. She is shot by a burst of machine-gun fire.

9b. Dogsborough's country house
Old Dogsborough is seen writing his will and confession, accusing the gangsters of all their misdeeds and himself of complicity in them.

Scene 10. Ui's suite at the Mammoth Hotel
The gangsters are forging a will in which Dogsborough distributes the various positions of authority between them. However quarrels break out about who should acquire what and accusations fly. Roma and his bodyguards pull guns on Givola and Giri. Announcing new plans and demanding they have faith in him, Ui remains in control. Giri and Givola exit. Ui tells Roma he intends to start up protection rackets in other towns including Cicero. Roma suspects that the Trust, supported by Giri and Givola, are plotting to keep Ui and Roma out of the Cicero business by exposing Ui in Dogsborough's will. Ui and Roma decide to liquidate the conspirators. Ui prepares the speech he is going to make to Roma's men.

Giri and Clark bring Betty Dullfeet, a Cicero greengrocer and wife of a newspaper magnate who has run anti-gangster stories in his paper, to meet Ui. They want Roma, now notorious for his murders, to be kept out of the Cicero deal and removed. Ui stands by his friend, Roma.

Sign 9 and 10: The impending death of the aged Hindenburg provokes bitter struggles in the Nazi camp. The Junkers and industrialists demand Röhm's removal. The occupation of Austria is planned.

Scene 11. A garage
Roma and his men await Ui so that together they can take action against the conspirators. Roma is ready to lay down his life for Ui. Ui enters with Givola. Roma's bodyguards and then Roma himself are killed. Ui has gone over to the conspirators and the Trust.

Sign 11: On the night of 30 June 1934 Hitler overpowers his friend Röhm at an inn where Röhm has been waiting for him. Up to the last moment Röhm thinks that Hitler is coming to arrange for a joint strike against Hindenburg and Göring.

Scene 12. Givola's flower shop
Betty Dullfeet, together with her husband, Ignatius, visits Givola's flower shop. Betty is ready to be won over to a merger with the Trust and Ui, and Dullfeet finally allows himself to be persuaded to stop his newspaper's anti-gangster policy.

Sign 12: Under compulsion the Austrian Chancellor Engelbert Dollfuss agrees to stop the attacks on Hitler that have been appearing in the Austrian press.

Scene 13. Outside the Cicero funeral chapel
In spite of their agreement, Dullfeet is murdered by the gangsters and buried with great pomp. He had kept silent but not spoken out in their favour. Outside the chapel Ui tries to convince Betty of his innocence and his friendship. Betty swears eternal enmity and refuses to have any business dealings with him.

Sign 13: Dollfuss is murdered at Hitler's instigation, but Hitler goes on negotiating with Austrian rightist circles.

Scene 14. Ui's bedroom at the Mammoth Hotel
In his sleep, Ui is haunted by the ghost of Roma, warning him that as he has betrayed so he will be betrayed. Ui awakes and orders his bodyguards to shoot at the ghost, which disappears.

Scene 15. The financial district
Summoned by Ui, the greengrocers of Chicago and Cicero assemble. In their discussions they deny any responsibility for Ui's rise to power and hope that someone else can stand up to him. Clark announces a merger between the Trust and the vegetable trade of Cicero. Betty Dullfeet advises the tradesmen of Cicero to recognise Ui. A shot is heard when one man leaves. The tradesmen decide to support Ui. The gangster proclaims the imminent conquest of many cities.

Sign 15: On 11 March 1938 Hitler marches into Austria. An election under the Nazi terror results in a 98% vote for Hitler.

Epilogue
An epilogue points out that such men can gain power at any time if we fail to act against them.

Commentary

Who was Bertolt Brecht?

Throughout his life Brecht challenged accepted conventions and attitudes, in his personal, political and theatrical lives. He is one of the seminal figures in twentieth-century theatre and yet remains a problematic character because there are so many contradictions evident in his actions and pronouncements. It seems impossible to pin him down absolutely – just when you think you know exactly what he intends, you will find a conflicting element.

When Brecht died, shortly before midnight on 14 August 1956 in his flat in East Berlin, he was a world-famous playwright and director. He was an extremely important figure in the new German Democratic Republic (GDR), the communist state that had been established in the Soviet occupation zone of Germany in October 1949 and was dissolved in October 1990. Brecht had thought very carefully about how he wanted to be buried. He chose, within a graveyard near to his own flat, a grave a few metres away from that of the philosopher Hegel, the father of 'dialectics' – the view of discourse in terms of thesis/antithesis and their interaction, which provided the philosophical underpinnings for Marxism and was also central to Brecht's literary work. The day after a private funeral attended only by family, close friends and colleagues, came the official state ceremony, at which the GDR's most important political and cultural figures almost queued up to pay tribute to Brecht.

This would have delighted Brecht who had always carefully courted publicity and cultivated his image. Equally he had cast himself as being 'different' from everybody else in the ways he sought to impress those who could give him access to the literary scene. The novelist, Lion

Feuchtwanger, recalled the impact of his first meeting with Brecht:

> He was slight, badly shaved, shabbily dressed. He stayed close to the walls, spoke with a Swabian accent, had written a play, was called Bertolt Brecht. The play was called *Spartacus*.
>
> Most young authors presenting a manuscript point out that they have torn this work from their bleeding hearts: but this young man emphasised that he had written *Spartacus* purely in order to make money.
>
> (*Brecht: As They Knew Him*, ed. Hubert Witt, trans. John Peet, International Publishers, New York, 1974, p. 17)

This play, which Brecht renamed at Feuchtwanger's suggestion *Drums in the Night*, provided Brecht's breakthrough into the literary world. It won Brecht the coveted Kleist Prize, making him one of the most widely known literary figures in Germany at the time (1922) and effectively launching his career which would span the next three and a half decades.

Throughout his adult life Brecht maintained a strong conviction of his own genius. He was determined to keep control over the ways his plays were performed, largely because he was convinced that most theatre directors had no understanding of what he was trying to accomplish. The ways in which he interfered in stage productions, which frequently involved hurling insults at actors and directors, did not always win him friends. But ultimately his insistence on doing things his way or not at all usually paid off.

Important figures in Brecht's life

His collaborators: Brecht liked to work collectively and throughout most of his professional life he collaborated with a succession of women who typed his manuscripts, helped him to develop his ideas and contributed to the writing of his plays. Before 1933 this role fell to Elisabeth Hauptmann, who edited Brecht's *Collected Works* after his death. During his years in exile in Scandinavia, his closest companion was Margarete Steffin who worked with Brecht on the manuscripts of his finest plays, such as *Life of Galileo* and *Mother Courage and her Children*, as well as *Arturo Ui*. 'Grete' Steffin's death from tuberculosis in 1941 in Moscow on the journey from Finland to the United States affected Brecht very deeply. Her place was taken by Ruth Berlau who went to the States with Brecht and also returned to post-war Berlin with him. These three women served Brecht with remarkable devotion – a devotion not always reciprocated. Without them, particularly Margarete Steffin, some of his finest work might not have been written.

His composers: From the outset Brecht's songs became an essential component of his plays. At first he composed the tunes himself but then he began working with professional musicians. He worked principally with three composers: Kurt Weill for six years (1927–33) Hanns Eisler for two lengthy periods, separated by Eisler's departure to the USA (1929–38, 1949–56), and Paul Dessau for the last phase of his life (1946–56). Whilst working with Weill and Eisler, up to 1938, Brecht and the composers were true collaborators, with the musical component of plays such as *Happy End* and *The Threepenny Opera* being integral to the text, giving a distinctive sound and flavour to the productions. However, although Brecht retained close contact with Eisler during his own exile in America, they did not work closely together from 1938 onwards. The plays written during this time, including *Arturo Ui*, were written without any integral musical component. Brecht's working arrangements with Eisler and Dessau from 1946 were not at the same collaborative level; from 1936 to the end of his life, no Brecht play bears a composer's name among the 'collaborators' listed after its title.

His wife: Helene Weigel, Brecht's second wife, held the most important place in his life. She was not involved in the writing of his plays but many of his parts were written with her in mind and her acting influenced the ways in which Brecht conceived of his plays on stage. Throughout the years of exile and when they returned to Germany, Weigel managed the Brecht household – a difficult task given the constant stream of visitors and the journeying from one country to another. After Brecht's death, Weigel ran the Berliner Ensemble theatre. She died in 1971.

Stage designer: Caspar Neher, Brecht's boyhood friend, became a celebrated stage designer whose often stark, innovative sets have become a hallmark of Brechtian theatre. He designed sets for productions of *In the Jungle of the Cities* (1923), *Edward II* (1924), *Baal* (1926) and *The Threepenny Opera* (1928), among others. His settings used gradations of subdued colours and brilliant stage lighting in the spirit of the play being performed. In 1948 after the war, he rejoined forces with Brecht, designing the set for *Antigone* in Switzerland. He designed *Mr Puntila and his Man Matti* (1949) and *Life of Galileo* in 1957 for the Berliner Ensemble.

It is important to realise that Brecht did not regard his written manuscript as the finished product. What counted was what was performed on stage. Brecht was a compulsive reviser. He was always willing to alter his plays when he saw how they worked on stage. Therefore the influence of Weigel and Neher, in particular, was not a matter of a few afterthoughts but a central part of Brecht's methods of production. Because *Arturo Ui* was not performed during Brecht's lifetime the play did not undergo the same redrafting process as Brecht's most highly regarded works.

Brecht's politics

Born into a well-to-do bourgeois family in the Bavarian city of Augsburg, Brecht lived through two world wars, the rise and fall of the most murderous and brutal dictatorship, and the division of his country – a historical context that framed his phenomenal literary output. During the First World War Brecht became a medical student at the University of Munich and then, from October 1918 to January 1919, served as an orderly at a clinic for soldiers with venereal disease. He witnessed the revolutionary upheavals of early 1919 in Munich but was more interested in the theatre and women. He seems to have played no coherent political role at all, more concerned with being an angry young man out to shock respectable bourgeois society.

During the early 1920s he was greatly influenced by Expressionism and the experimental theatre of the time. However, in 1926, Brecht, while researching material for a play about the Chicago grain exchange, discovered the writings of Karl Marx and the theory of dialectics. The play was never completed but in Marx Brecht found what he regarded as the key to understanding the world around him and to the historical process, as well as a framework and structure for his own writing. Brecht's work became didactic, seeking to teach and encourage active thought by the audience. For Brecht, the task became the tearing away of surface appearances to expose the true nature of society.

Despite his commitment to Marxist ideology and the explicitly left-wing nature of many of his plays, Brecht never joined the Communist Party. At the same time the success of his plays made him famous and earned him a good living. During his exile from Germany he lived comfortably despite his unsuccessful attempts to sell scripts in Hollywood or to get his plays performed in New York. During his time in the USA he was hauled before the House Committee on Un-American Activities accused of being a member of the Communist Party. Brecht proved himself a master of ambiguity and political survival with his cleverly crafted replies. When he returned to his native land, he did settle in the Soviet Communist sector of East Berlin but perhaps a major attraction was that he was given a theatre there. It is interesting to note that after his return to Berlin, Brecht did not write any more plays – he concentrated on putting into practice a new style of theatre.

Even when he lived in a state which officially sanctioned Marxism, Brecht remained a controversial figure, since his style of epic theatre was at odds with the official Stalinist line of Socialist Realism. Brecht ensured that he kept his options open by having an Austrian passport which allowed him to travel freely in the West and he also maintained his contacts with his West German publisher, Peter Suhrkamp.

In June 1953 there was an uprising of workers against the GDR government. Brecht did not openly support either side, although the content of his plays would perhaps lead us to expect that he would have supported the workers. Instead he adopted a critical and ambiguous stance of solidarity with the government. He wrote a letter to the party leader in which he affirmed his loyal allegiance to the Socialist Unity Party but then afterwards wrote a sharply satirical poem in which he attacked the actions of the GDR. It seemed impossible to pin down exactly where Brecht's loyalties lay. Equally confusing, given Brecht's intense opposition to fascism, was his failure to voice any criticism of the Stalinist regime in the USSR (and GDR). He alienated many in the West by his acceptance of the Stalin Peace Prize in 1955.

Brecht's views on theatre

Brecht came to public notice as an opponent of the then fashionable theatre of illusion as characterised by the work of Max Reinhardt, but he was also opposed to the expressionist approach which emphasised overt, declamatory demonstrations of feelings. He drew up a rough-and-ready yet basic distinction between the old Aristotelian theatre, which he generally called 'dramatic' and associated with the social dramas of Ibsen, and his own new theatre which he called 'epic' and on which his theories and practice – especially with his own company the Berliner Ensemble – were based. From the beginning of his career Brecht had fought a running battle against the conventional theatre of his day, labelling it as 'culinary' because, like good cooking, it satisfied the senses but did not engage the mind. For the production of one of his first plays, *Drums in the Night* in 1922, he had banners put up in the auditorium telling the audience not to 'gawp so romantically' and in his essay in 1935, 'On Experimental Theatre', Brecht asked:

> How can the theatre be entertaining and at the same time instructive? How can it be taken out of the traffic in intellectual drugs and transformed from a place of illusion to a place of insight?

For Brecht the traditional or dramatic theatre was a place where the audience was absorbed into a comforting illusion which played on its emotions and left its members drained, but with a sense of satisfaction which predisposed them to accept the world as it was. What he himself was looking for was a theatre that would help to change the world.

The term 'epic' was in use in German debates before Brecht adapted it, and he drew on several sources in generating his own interpretation:

> the political theatre of Erwin Piscator and German agitprop; the cabaret of Frank Wedekind and the work of the music hall comedian Karl Valentin; Charlie Chaplin and the American silent film; Asian and revolutionary Soviet theatre; as well as Shakespeare and Elizabethan chronicle plays.
>
> (Peter Brooker, 'Key Words in Brecht's Theory and Practice' in *The Cambridge Companion to Brecht*, ed. Thomson and Sacks, Cambridge, 1994)

He first set out his ideas on epic theatre in his 'Notes on the Opera *The Rise and Fall of the City of Mahagonny*', where he listed the main characteristics of 'dramatic' and 'epic' theatre, insisting, however, that the contrasts he was highlighting were not absolute but rather a matter of emphasis. Although the following table gives a good starting point for a consideration of Brecht's theory and practice, it should be noted that Brecht in conducting his campaign to change the dominant mode of theatre, tended at this point to overstress the differences, for example the contrast between 'feeling' and 'reason' he never took to be absolute. He knew perfectly well that plenty of 'dramatic' plays arouse thought and that in his own 'epic' plays feeling was by no means excluded. It is therefore important to recognise the element of tactical exaggeration in the way he presents his table of differences.

Dramatic theatre	Epic theatre
plot	narrative
implicates the spectator in a stage situation	turns the spectator into an observer but
wears down his capacity for action	arouses his capacity for action
provides him with sensations	forces him to take decisions
experience	picture of the world
the spectator is involved in something	he is made to face something
suggestion	argument
instinctive feelings are preserved	brought to the point of recognition
the spectator is in the thick of it, shares the experience	the spectator stands outside, studies
the human being is taken for granted	the human being is the object of the enquiry
he is unalterable	he is alterable and able to alter
eyes on the finish	eyes on the course
one scene makes another	each scene for itself
growth	montage
linear development	in curves
evolutionary determinism	jumps
man as a fixed point	man as a process
thought determines being	social being determines thought
feeling	reason

(*Brecht on Theatre*, p. 37)

In drawing up this list Brecht challenged traditional ways of classifying texts. The term 'dramatic' is usually associated with texts written for performance where the characters and settings represented in the writing are limited by the conventions and resources of the theatre. The length of a piece of dramatic writing is also limited by the audience's patience and concentration so that dramatists are effectively restricted to presenting a unified plot which shows a conflict and its resolution.

The term 'epic', on the other hand, associated with the epics of Homer (*The Odyssey*) and Virgil (*The Aeneid*), indicates work on a grand scale, illustrating the story of a whole society. It has normally been used about novels, indicating that the author is recounting a story using as many episodes as is necessary to contain his complete story. The term 'epic theatre' was first used in Germany during the 1920s and is now firmly associated with Brecht (and his friend and collaborator Erwin Piscator). Epic theatre cuts across traditional divisions. Brecht found in epic writing an objectivity, an ability of the author to stand back and comment on the action, which attracted him. He wanted to make his audience think, not just feel; to find ways of thinking that would enable them to apply those processes to their real worlds and therefore act as a force for change in society. And yet Brecht's plays, whilst laying bare the wider concerns of mankind, are constructed around characters whose stature is essentially small in relation to their social and historical contexts.

In moving away from the conventional dramatic theatre, Brecht's first change of emphasis was in the manner in which events were presented to the audience. Instead of involving the audience, persuading them to suspend their disbelief and become immersed in the lives of the characters as they unfolded before them, Brecht strove to ensure that his audience retained their critical judgement. He wanted the audience to observe objectively what was happening, aware of the alternatives that could have been followed. Whereas the plot of a play for the dramatic theatre depended upon closely intermeshed scenes that evolved apparently inexorably one from the other, the epic theatre presented scenes which moved in curves and jumps, making the audience think critically about what was unfolding before them.

In an essay written in 1936 but unpublished in his lifetime, Brecht distinguished between the spectator's attitude in the dramatic and epic theatres:

> The dramatic theatre's spectator says: Yes, I have felt like that too – Just like me – It's only natural – It'll never change – The sufferings of this man appal me, because they are inescapable – That's great art; it all seems the most obvious thing in the world – I weep when they weep, I laugh when they laugh.
>
> The epic theatre's spectator says: I'd never have thought it – That's not the way – That's extraordinary, hardly believable – It's got to stop – The sufferings of this man appal me, because they are unnecessary – That's great art; nothing obvious in it – I laugh when they weep, I weep when they laugh.
>
> (*Brecht on Theatre*, p. 71)

In order to achieve these objectives Brecht devised particular dramatic techniques which characterise his scripts and informed the productions of his plays, particularly as performed by the Berliner Ensemble. The text of *Arturo Ui* exemplifies many such Brechtian devices.

Brecht was a very practical man who wrote plays with their production in mind. He was always prepared to modify or scrap ideas if they didn't work. Nevertheless understanding Brecht's theories is vital if a full understanding of his aims, intentions and achievements is to be arrived at. Avoiding the theory can lead to Brecht's innovations appearing to be just a series of technical gimmicks. In a statement made near the end of his life Brecht summed up his aims:

> My whole theory is much naiver than people think, or than my way of

putting it allows them to suppose. Perhaps I can excuse myself by pointing to the case of Albert Einstein, who told the physicist Infield that ever since boyhood he had merely reflected on the man running after a ray of light and the man shut in a descending lift. And think what complications that led to! I wanted to take the principle that it was not just a matter of interpreting the world but of changing it, and apply that to the theatre.

(*Brecht on Theatre*, p. 248)

Two points are worth noting here: firstly, that 'naive' is not a pejorative term to Brecht; his aim was to make drama simpler, to cut away confusions and complications. Secondly, Brecht's guiding principle was drawn from Marx's *Theses on Feuerbach*: 'The philosophers so far have only interpreted the world; the point, however, is to change it.'

From this key principle emerge some of the most important of Brecht's theatrical intentions:

- Since the world is all the time changing and capable of being changed, the playwright must neither assume nor allow his audience to assume that any phenomenon or activity is eternally obvious or uninteresting. The interest is in not just what happens but how and why. The playwright's job is to make the ordinary seem extraordinary by letting us see in a new way what we tend to dismiss as obvious.
- Brecht believed that audiences needed to be surprised because what they took for granted about life and the world was not necessarily unimportant or inevitable but was what they had been conditioned (usually unconsciously) to take for granted. The conditioning was done (again not necessarily consciously) by those who held power.
- His constant emphasis was that the audience should be actively critical rather than passively receptive of the play. He wanted to

use drama to help the audience to establish new ways of acting upon their 'real' world. He wanted to get rid of the ritual element in drama which involved submission to outside forces rather than an attempt to assess, criticise and control those forces.

- This meant that Brecht used his plays to weaken the hold of certain tendencies and ideas – such as fascism – and to strengthen others. In the struggle between classes, he was on the side of the working class.

- The objectivity inherent in this approach meant that the audience could understand the actions and emotions of a given character and then be able think about why such a character has behaved in such a way in that situation or why the situation has arisen. In opposing the established Aristotelian view of tragedy, in which the spectator participates in the drama and is purged of emotions by way of the pity and terror which the acting on stage evokes, Brecht challenged the view of the world in which men and women have little control over their destinies. Brecht's approach grew from and embodied his view of life as a struggle for emancipation, to enable the audience not to submit to power which is outside themselves and manipulates them for ends which are not theirs.

- Brecht also understood the need for drama to be entertaining – but he thought nothing was greater fun than finding out new things. He wanted to demystify the processes surrounding theatrical activity.

Brecht's intention was to develop a dialectical relationship with the audience, an interactive relationship involving the audience in consciously considering the situations and alternatives faced by the stage characters. Whereas the actor in naturalist theatre focused on the stage itself, the Brechtian actor's focus was the audience. His stage characters are not necessarily believable. In Brecht's plays it is not the actor's job to generate sympathy for, or antipathy towards, a character; their actions are to be examined critically from an emotional distance.

There are three key terms which Brecht coined to describe particular aspects of his epic or, as he later termed it, dialectical theatre:

Gest (or Gestus)

The development of the idea of *Gestus* became an essential link between Brecht's theory of acting and his practice as a playwright. It is a difficult word to interpret. The original, now obsolete English word 'gest' meant 'bearing or carriage'. It would seem that Brecht wanted the one term to do a multiplicity of work. Brecht distinguished *Gestus* from gesture (*Geste*) by calling it

> a number of related gestures expressing such different attitudes as politeness, anger and so on.
>
> (*Brecht on Theatre*, p. 246)

but also stated that:

> A language is gestic when it is grounded in a gest and conveys particular attitudes adopted by the speaker towards other men.
>
> (ibid., p. 104)

and of a song in the didactic play *The Mother*:

> The piece 'In Praise of Learning', which links the problem of learning with that of the working class's accession to power, is infected by the music with a heroic yet naturally cheerful gest.
>
> (ibid., p. 88)

and again:

> The realm of attitudes adopted by the characters towards one another is

what we call the realm of gest.

(ibid., p. 198)

Trying to tie down a precise definition seems a thankless task and Brecht himself only occasionally saw an actor capable of gestic acting. He notes these occasions: Peter Lorre in *Man equals Man*, Charles Laughton in some parts of *Life of Galileo*, Helene Weigel in *The Mother* and *Mother Courage*. It is true to say that perfect 'gestic' acting would allow the meaning of a scene to be obvious even to an audience of the deaf.

Arnold Kettle's explanation of *Gestus*, in Unit 24 of the Open University course A3047 Drama, provides a clear insight into this quicksilver term:

> To Brecht a play is a series of *gests*. 'Each single incident has its basic *gest*.' Splitting the material he has to offer into one *gest* after another, the actor masters his character by first mastering the 'story'. Everything hangs on the 'story' which is in effect 'the complete fitting together of all the *gestic* incidents': but though each *gest* is in this basic sense only meaningful as part of the 'story', it is through the series of *gests* that the 'story' is revealed.

Brecht wrote:

> Gest is not supposed to mean gesticulation: it is not a matter of explanatory or emphatic movements of the hands, but of overall attitudes.
>
> (*Brecht on Theatre*, p. 104)

Kettle goes on to draw a link with the English word 'gist':

> The idea of *gest* also includes the notion that the text itself has to be seen as action and gesture, not as disembodied words. There is a sort of pun here with our own word 'gist'. The *gest*, you might say expresses the dialectical gist of the situation the dramatist is presenting.

Verfremdung

The translation of this term has also proved difficult. It has
sometimes been translated as 'alienation' but another German word
Entfremdung is normally used to mean this and has a range of
meanings which do not match Brecht's intentions in using
Verfremdung. Basically the *Verfremdungseffekt* is Brecht's means of
controlling his audience's response so that they do not lose
themselves emotionally in the action but are forced into a critical,
thinking awareness. The effect is partly achieved by the author's
text itself, partly through the director's handling of the text and
partly through the actors' attitudes to what they are doing.

The text itself:

• Setting the text in the past distances it.
• Avoiding rhetorical language except in very special circumstances
  (e.g. Arturo Ui's speeches).
• Constructing the whole play in the form of a story (epic) as
  opposed to giving it the structure of an individual's emotional
  crisis.

The director's approach:

• The stage is treated strictly as a stage. The curtain should not
  conceal everything (e.g. scene shifting) but should allow the
  audience to be aware that work is going on. Lights are not
  concealed. The illusion that is created must always be recognised
  as an illusion so that reality is turned into art and can be seen to
  be alterable.
• A summary of the action of the scene about to be presented may
  be projected on a screen before the scene.
• Filmstrips, videos, projections may be used for purposes of
  background, information and to link stage events with reality.
• The setting in terms of the whole stage picture is important
  because it creates an illusion and yet limits its essential elements.

- Open use of technology and stage mechanics (e.g. revolving stage) can assist the *V-effekt*.
- All of the details presented on stage are realistic – much more trouble is taken to get these absolutely right than may be the case for naturalistic plays. This is shown clearly in the opening lines of Brecht's poem 'Weigel's props':

> Just as the millet farmer picks out for his trial plot
> The heaviest seeds and the poet
> The exact words for his verse so
> She selects the objects to accompany
> Her characters across the stage.
>
> (trans. John Willett, *Poems 1913–1956*, p. 427)

The songs: Although integrated into the text, songs are performed within a convention different from that of the rest of the play. The singers, Brecht explained, were openly 'the playwright's own accomplices', using the 'sister art' to make points which could not be made in the same way within the normal text.

The actors: The Brechtian actor is trained not to 'immerse himself' in his part but to understand it and its role in the social situation depicted by the play. This does not mean that the actor does not think himself into his part but it does mean that he is discouraged from becoming possessed by it. The task of a Brechtian actor is to understand and communicate, not to empathise and be transformed. This point is made clearly in Brecht's poem, 'The moment before impact':

> I speak my lines before
> The audience hears them; what they will hear is
> Something done with. Every word that leaves the lip
> Describes an arc, and then
> Falls on the listener's ear; I wait and hear

The way it strikes; I know
We are not feeling the same thing and
We are not feeling it at the same time.
   (trans. Edith Anderson, *Poems 1913–1956*, p. 342)

Clear contrasts are evident with the naturalistic Stanislavskian approach. These differences can be clearly seen in Brecht's response to what he cited as a typically 'naturalistic' description by the actor Rapaport:

> On the stage the actor is surrounded entirely by fictions ... The actor must be able to regard all this as though it were true, as though he were convinced that all that surrounds him on stage is a living reality and, along with himself, he must convince the audience as well. This is the central feature of our method of work on the part ... Take any object, a cap for example; lay it on the table or on the floor and try to regard it as though it were a rat: make believe that it is a rat, not a cap ... Picture what sort of rat it is; what size, colour? ... We thus commit ourselves to believe quite naively that the object before us is something other than it is and, at the same time, learn to compel the audience to believe.
>
>   (*Brecht on Theatre*, p. 142)

Brecht rejected this approach outright:

> This might be thought to be a course of instruction for conjurers but in fact it is a course of acting, supposedly according to Stanislavsky's method. One wonders if a technique that equips an actor to make an audience see rats where there aren't any can really be all that suitable for disseminating the truth. Given enough alcohol it doesn't take acting to persuade almost anybody that he is seeing rats: pink ones.

In battling against the 'culinary' theatre, Brecht sought to establish a realist approach. In an essay 'The Popular and the Realistic', he set out a list of criteria for his definition of realism:

Brecht's criteria	Interpretation
Laying bare society's causal network	Showing the audience the ways in which human action is determined by people's social positions and expectations
Showing up the dominant viewpoint as the viewpoint of the dominators	Revealing that what are assumed to be eternal truths are simply views that reinforce the power of those in power
Writing from the standpoint of the class which has prepared the broadest solutions for the most pressing problems afflicting human society	Championing the working class by showing their capacity to resolve basic issues of survival
Emphasising the dynamics of development	Revealing the nature of the relationship between one action and another
Concrete and so as to encourage abstraction	Creating specific characters and stories played in such a way as to make the audience think

Brecht was intensely aware of the ways in which what is familiar protects itself from criticism by its unobtrusiveness. The *Verfremdungseffekte* were designed to expose the familiar – Brecht's actors were to present things in their concrete reality so that the audience would be encouraged to think about what had given rise to the situation depicted and therefore consider ways to change those conditions in future.

Montage
Brecht's concept of 'epic' involved the principle of montage, of creating a play which showed one thing after another and where each scene existed for itself; where the links between events were

deliberately severed, generating a series of isolated images which the audience had to work to connect. A performance would be broken down into clearly marked segments.

Montage theory had been developed by Russian and American film makers, perhaps most explicitly by the Soviet film director, Sergei Eisenstein. The term first appeared in his 1923 essay 'Montazh attraktsionov' (Montage of Attractions). It referred to the circus-style series of episodic 'turns' which characterised his re-worked version of Ostrovsky's nineteenth-century classic *Enough Stupidity in Every Wise Man*, staged as a satirico-political clown show, with acrobatics, high-wire stunts and filmed inserts. He later adapted his ideas to the editing of film – the intercutting and juxtaposition of unrelated but emotive images which produce a heightened political perception in the observer. Probably the most famous example is the 'Odessa Steps' sequence in *Battleship Potemkin* where Eisenstein intercut the image of stamping military boots with pictures of a pram, containing a baby, falling down the steps. In the original manifesto, an 'attraction' was defined as

> any aggressive moment in theatre, i.e. any element of it that subjects the audience to emotional or psychological influence, verified by experience and mathematically calculated to produce specific emotional shocks in the spectator in their proper order within the whole. These shocks provide the only opportunity of perceiving the ideological aspect of what is being shown, the final ideological conclusion.

Eisenstein pointed out that if one fragment of a woman dressed in black is shown and that fragment is followed by another, a photo of a grave, the viewer of these two discreet fragments would then mentally telescope them into an image of a widow. In other words, the spectator provides continuity. Earlier, the American director, D.W. Griffith, had introduced a technique of film cutting that jumped from scene to scene deliberately leaving out segments of the action and relying on the spectator to make an unbroken transition from Scene A to B to C and so on. Brecht insisted that Peter Lorre in the 1931 production of *Man equals Man* adopt a style of acting that created this montage technique. When Lorre's performance was criticised for being exaggerated, disjointed and impersonal – for example when Lorre was supposed to express chalk-white fear at the prospect of his imminent execution, he turned his back on the audience, dipped his hands in a bowl of white chalk, smeared it on his face, and abruptly turned again to confront the audience – Brecht leapt to his defence, arguing that the unity of type or character in the role came about 'despite, or rather by means of interruptions and jumps'. Responding to the challenge that Peter Lorre was 'short-winded and episodic', Brecht replied that the actor 'links all these single episodes together and absorbs them in the combined flow of his role'. Lorre was attempting to match the stress on breaks with stress on continuity. It is important to remember that Brecht's plays are crafted in such a way as to ensure that the breaks are always offset by carefully structured elements to establish their continuity and build bridges across the gaps.

Thus montage can be seen as a crucial element in challenging the audience to think, to make connections and to realise the need for action beyond the theatre.

> The stage began to be instructive.
>
> Oil, inflation, war, social struggles, the family, religion, wheat, the meat market, all became subjects for theatrical representation. Choruses enlightened the spectator. . . . Films showed a montage of events from all over the world. Projections added statistical material. And as the 'background' came to the front of the stage so people's activity was subjected to criticism . . . The theatre became an affair for philosophers, but only such philosophers as wished not just to explain but also to change it.
>
> (*Brecht on Theatre*, pp. 71–2)

Parallels – historical, literary, the American hoodlum

The rise of Hitler

Brecht wrote *Arturo Ui* in Finland in about three weeks in March
and April 1941, while waiting for a visa to travel to the USA. The
play is a parody exposing the ways in which Hitler was allowed to
come to power and wreak so much devastation. Brecht added the
Epilogue after the end of the Second World War, emphasising the
final and most important lesson – that we must all be forever
vigilant in ensuring that life and breath are not given to those such
as Hitler.

Although the play has resonance across all times and peoples,
there is no doubt that an appreciation of the particular situation
informing Brecht's writing and providing the stimulus to create the
play, lends an additional layer of understanding to Brecht's
intentions. The Germany of Brecht's lifetime was significantly
different from the modern Germany of today. When Brecht was
born in 1898, Germany had been a unified country for less than
thirty years.

A brief historical background

1815–71: In 1815 at the end of the Napoleonic Wars, four nations,
Russia, France, Prussia and Austria, were of roughly equal power
in Europe, ensuring a balance of power that helped to maintain
peace. Germany did not exist as a unified country: it was just a
loose confederation of small independent states. However, in 1862,
Bismarck was appointed Prussian prime minister and set out to
unite the German states under Prussia's leadership. Having
appointed Helmuth von Moltke to reorganise the army, he defeated
Austria and then turned on France. The Franco-Prussian War
ended in 1871 with the signing of the Treaty of Frankfurt by
which the French provinces of Alsace and Lorraine were ceded to
Germany. William I of Prussia created the new German Reich

(Empire) by uniting the German kingdoms of the North German Confederation and the South German States. For the first time Germany was a unified country with Bismarck at its helm as Chancellor. France was no longer a major power. To the Germans their new-found status was a cause of enormous celebration, with the soldiers being lauded as heroes.

1890–1918: In 1890 Bismarck was dismissed by Kaiser Wilhelm II, a vain, boastful man who loved pomp and ceremony and longed to be popular. Where Bismarck had been a clever politician who knew that he had to isolate France in order to ensure that she could not find allies to help her take revenge against Germany for the defeat of 1871, Wilhelm II appointed less able ministers who failed to prevent Russia signing a Dual Entente with France. When the First World War broke out, Germany, allied with Austria, seized the opportunity to declare war on both France and Russia. As part of the plan to attack France, the Kaiser's army invaded Belgium, breaking the agreement with Britain on Belgian neutrality embodied in the Treaty of London in 1839. This drew Britain into the war on 4 August 1914. Over the next four years the war extended over thirty countries. The war ended at 11am on 11 November 1918. A new German republican government was installed, the Emperor having abdicated. Hitler served as a corporal in the German army and never forgave the humiliation, as he saw it, of the Treaty of Versailles in 1919.

1918–30: Having been defeated in the First World War, Germany was faced with the task of rebuilding its economy. By 1929 the world depression, which had started in the USA, hit Germany with awful force. Every European country was affected but Germany was in the worst position because its rebuilding had been financed by loans of 7 billion US dollars. Inflation was rampant. The loans stopped; wages fell; factories and businesses closed. In 1920 Hitler formed the National Socialist German Workers' Party (Nazis) with a gymnastics and sports division known as the Storm-troopers. They exploited the genuine anger and despair of many Germans, turning it into brutality. On 23 November 1923 Hitler tried to engineer what he called a 'National Revolution' but his unsuccessful 'putsch' ended with sixteen Nazis and three policemen dead. Hitler was arrested and sentenced to five years' imprisonment but in fact was released after nine months.

In 1929 there were 1,320,000 unemployed in Germany. By 1932 there were 5,102,000. In this climate of national misery, Hitler found the perfect conditions for growth for his Nazi Party and his own ambitions. Hindenburg, who was a hero to the German people because of his successes as a general during the First World War, became the President of Germany in 1925.

Arturo Ui *in the historical context*

Brecht's play exposes the ease with which a monstrous criminal can exploit the fears and greed of those with financial and political power in a period of instability. It acts as a warning that any such circumstances can result in such an outcome; it warns against the complacency of believing that the events of the Hitler era could never be repeated at another time in another place.

The play itself is a montage of self-contained scenes, after many of which Brecht includes a piece of text to be projected in the theatre, naming the historical event to which the particular scene alludes. These historical parallels need to be understood if the play is to have its full effect. Brecht's own list of these parallels gives no explanations since at the time he wrote the play the events were far more recent and therefore a common knowledge could be assumed. For some critics, one of the problems of guaranteeing the full impact of Brecht's intentions on a modern audience may be the unlikelihood of a clear knowledge of the historical events being parodied.

Brecht's own list of parallels		Amplifying explanations of names and events
The play	*Life*	
Dogsborough	Hindenburg	Field-marshal in WWI. President of Germany 1925–33
Ui	Hitler	Adolf Hitler, founder of National Socialist German Workers' Party (Nazis) in 1920. Chancellor of Germany 1933
Giri	Göring	Hermann Göring, head of the Nazi airforce
Roma	Röhm	Ernst Röhm, head of the Nazi storm-troopers (Brown Shirts)
Givola	Goebbels	Josef Goebbels, Nazi propaganda minister, an ex-journalist
Dullfeet	Dollfuss	Chancellor of Austria 1932–34, murdered by SS men
Cauliflower Trust	Junkers	Prussian landowners. Prussia, formerly one of the four most powerful countries in Europe, was a rich industrialised region in the north-east of Germany
Vegetable traders	Petty bourgeoisie	Middle-class tradespeople who supported Hitler by failing to oppose his policies and actions because they were frightened of the potential power of the workers

Dock aid scandal	*Osthilfe* scandal	A political scandal involving Hindenburg, the German President, in which he accepted a gift of land as a bribe from the Junkers. Hitler used knowledge of this to blackmail Hindenburg into supporting him
Warehouse fire trial	Reichstag fire trial	In February 1933, the Reichstag, the seat of the legislature in Berlin, burned down. It is now alleged that the Nazis started the fire themselves giving them the opportunity to take action against their enemies. A jobless Dutchman, van der Lubbe, was sentenced to death by the highest court although he seems to have been drunk/drugged throughout the trial
Chicago	Germany	Chicago was the headquarters of Al Capone
Cicero	Austria	Capone moved into Cicero, a suburb of Chicago, on 1 April 1924; Austria was Hitler's birthplace and the first country his army invaded

Additional parallels	
Mrs Dullfeet	The Austrian people whom Hitler courted
Clark	Franz von Papen – landowner and industrialist who became German Chancellor in 1932 and helped to pave the way for Hitler

Killing of Roma	The Night of the Long Knives, 30 June 1934 – Hitler ordered the execution of Röhm and other leaders of the Brown Shirts by members of the Nazi Party

On 11 March 1938 Hitler marched into Austria. This was the first of his incursions into other countries. He then invaded Czechoslovakia, Poland, Denmark, Norway, the Netherlands, Belgium, Luxembourg, France, Yugoslavia, Greece, the Soviet Union and others.

Literary parallels and references

The play is concerned with one particular and limited part of the history of Hitler's rise to power. Certainly, as some critics have been quick to point out, it does not deal with Hitler's atrocious treatment of other races, particularly the Jews, but concentrates on exposing Hitler's opportunism and manipulation of complex circumstances during a specific period of his rise to power. It acts as Brecht's warning to the audience of how easily such individuals can exploit the corruption innate, in Brecht's view, in capitalist political life, in other words that fascism is a dangerously renewable force.

There are also several literary parallels and allusions used by Brecht in constructing *Arturo Ui*, giving the play a wealth of echoes which reinforce the sense and power of the evil personified by Ui. In the visit of Mr and Mrs Dullfeet to Givola's flower shop Brecht creates a direct parallel with a famous scene, set in a garden, from Goethe's *Faust*, where Mephistopheles softens up Martha while Faust is preparing the ground for Gretchen's ruin. Brecht alternates the appearance of the couples, Givola and Dullfeet and

Betty and Ui, just as Goethe scripts his scene. Gretchen's well-known line to Faust:

Now tell me, how do you feel about religion?

is parodied directly and extended by Brecht in the section of dialogue beginning:

What, Mr Ui, does religion mean to you?

Brecht was an avid reader of Shakespeare. Shakespeare's history plays influenced Brecht's development of his idea of epic theatre, with the emphasis on showing the ways in which a society is shaped by political and personal effects and interrelationships. Brecht also borrowed particular lines and scenes from Shakespeare. Like Shakespeare's Richard III, Arturo Ui woos and wins over the widow of the man he has murdered; and like Macbeth, has a nightmare vision in which he sees his victim, Roma. In the scene where the actor coaches Ui, Brecht draws again on Shakespeare in his use of Mark Antony's 'Friends, Romans and countrymen' speech from *Julius Caesar*. The impact of Ui's repetition of the line about Brutus is greater because of the echoes in the audience's minds of Brutus' extreme act of treachery.

The world of Al Capone and the American hoodlum

At the time of writing the play Brecht was fascinated by the world of American gangsters. He had visited America in 1935 and throughout his life read many books and articles on America, being a particular fan of American detective stories. In writing *Arturo Ui* he seems to have wanted to be able to tap into the culture of the country to which he was emigrating. Among the many American books Brecht possessed was F.D. Pasley's biography of Al Capone. Many details that appear in the play are found in that biography, for example:

Al Capone's headquarters, Chicago's Metropole Hotel	Ui's headquarters, Mammoth Hotel
St Valentine's Day Massacre in 1929 – Capone assassinated seven of Bugs Moran's gang in a warehouse	Shooting of Roma and his gang in a garage
Capone's use of florist shops as a cover	Use of Givola's flower shop
Capone took huge wreaths to funerals of opponents	Ui attends Dullfeet's funeral

Brecht was also greatly influenced by the increasingly popular world of the cinema. During his first visit to America in 1935 he had seen an enormous number of gangster films. He understood that cinema-goers tended to idolise the criminal, provided his crimes were on a big enough scale and committed with skill and daring. His favourite film actor was Charlie Chaplin who also caricatured the personality of Hitler in *The Great Dictator*, made in 1938.

The multi-layered references and parodies create a complexity that each member of the audience has to unravel, but at the same time generate a series of echoes that lend Brecht's 'historical gangster show' greater resonance. However, as a result of these many references and parallels as well as the central parody, the question arises as to whether the play stands alone on its own merits if a member of the audience does not have access to one or some of these points of reference. If we do not share the playwright's own perspective because of the problems of time and historical/literary knowledge, how much is lost in terms of theatrical impact? Can Brecht's aims for his epic theatre be achieved in such circumstances in relation to *Arturo Ui*?

Problems of reception

Although the play was written in 1941 (after the completion of *Mr Puntila* and *The Good Person of Szechwan*), it was never performed during Brecht's lifetime. Brecht wrote it with an American audience in mind and he did make attempts to get it staged when he first went to America. These efforts came to nothing and the play was put aside for other projects. However, Brecht did look at it again with a view to performance during 1953 but his discussions about the play with a group of writers seem to have made him doubt the advisability of staging *Ui* for a German audience. Brecht did not feel that they would be able to cope with seeing Hitler mocked. He stated that *Fear and Misery of the Third Reich* (which consists of a string of short, naturalistic scenes about life under the Nazis and would make the audience see exactly what was being mocked in *Ui*) would need to be staged first. The play was prepared for publication but its first performance was not until 1958 in Stuttgart, West Germany. In the same year it entered the repertoire of the Berliner Ensemble in a highly acclaimed production with Brecht's son-in-law, Ekkehard Schall, as Ui.

A glance at the reviews of the 1987 production with Griff Rhys Jones as Ui, shows many of the basic difficulties to be overcome in performance. Andrew Rissik in the *Independent* condemned the production's inability to 'darken the stage [metaphorically] so that our laughter freezes as he [Ui] speaks' and commented that:

> Brecht wrote the play in 1941 and, despite the razor edge of its comedy, his intentions can rarely have been less flippant. In its deft, light and joltingly funny way, *Arturo Ui* is anatomising the moral laziness and shortsighted self-interest whereby a society allows itself to be commandeered by a gang of malevolent mediocrities, whose only ambition is the spotlight of absolute power. The play's story is not the obvious, emotive one of the lunatics seizing control, but the more dispassionate political narrative which shows common sense and

intelligence bending to ferocious will power.

Robin Ray, reviewing the same production for *Punch*, opens his equally critical review with:

> At the Queen's Theatre we have Bertolt Brecht's *The Resistible Rise of Arturo Ui*. Take note of that word 'resistible' for it is the key to the author's theatrical philosophy – never assume your audience has enough brains to think for itself, they are here to be told (next ve haff 'Hedda sex-disgusts-me Gabler' zen 'Richard vat-a-bastard III'). Written in 1941, this play imparts the startling information that Adolf Hitler was a nasty piece of work which comes as no surprise to those of us on whom he was dropping bombs at the time.

Two eminent Brechtian scholars, Martin Esslin and Ronald Gray, were deeply critical of the use of allegory, Esslin finding it 'laboured' and Gray terming it 'flippant'. However, Brecht was not simply debunking the Great Dictator through ridicule, like Charlie Chaplin, but seeking to expose the historical forces that brought him to power. Esslin's objection that Brecht knew nothing about Chicago recalls many of the complaints about Shakespeare's lack of specific knowledge of his settings (for example, he gives Bohemia, a land-locked country, a coastline) but Esslin misses the point that Brecht's real scene is Germany.

As Keith Dickson in *Towards Utopia: a Study of Brecht* has carefully catalogued, there are many differences between the rise of Ui and the history of Hitler's rise to power. For those wishing to watch a carefully documented history of the period, this will be an enormous failing – but it was not Brecht's intention to present a factual history play. He wanted to expose the human greed and economic flaws endemic in the capitalist business system that allowed such a development. The point is to enable an audience to think about and begin to understand that they must act to ensure that such a thing never happens again. By focusing on the political rise of Hitler Brecht avoided the issues of the Holocaust and the suppression of races. Understandably this generated a sense of outrage in some of his critics who interpreted this as Brecht's failure to acknowledge the most profoundly inhuman acts perpetrated by the Nazis. In his own notes about *Ui* Brecht attempts to explain his focus but for many the play remains unacceptable.

Perhaps a key factor in that unacceptability is the humour of the play. Black though the comedy may be, it is still uproariously funny in performance – as can be gathered from the descriptions included of key moments from performances. The basic situation of Ui's wresting of power from the Trust, the slapstick caricatures, the jokes, the contrast between the form of the blank verse and the meaning of the words, all combine to create a bleakly simple but hilariously funny play which poses the dual question time and time again: how could the people of Chicago and the Cauliflower Trust/ the people of Germany and her politicians have allowed Arturo Ui/Hitler to rise? Why was that Rise not Resisted?

Interestingly, immediately after the trial which in seven short scenes, punctuated by music and blackout, conveys in a hilarious but horrific way the total corruption of the judicial process in Nazi Germany, Brecht inserts a tiny piece of realistic horror as a woman climbs out of a shot-up truck and screams for help. In microcosm the audience is shown the horror of the refusal to respond to people whose lives were literally being destroyed. This deliberate use of contrast shocks the members of the audience into silence as they are forced to realise the blame which the 'ordinary people' – themselves – share in ignoring the abuses of power which allowed such atrocities to occur.

As Jan Needle and Peter Thomson forcibly emphasise:

> The play is a comedy, a ruthlessly funny and vicious one, which mocks classical drama, as well as Hitler, and which shows up politicians, some of whom we chose to call statesmen, as shallow, unserious, cowardly, stupid ... The play is in fact *revolutionary*, in an entirely disreputable way; totally without respect for Hitler, it portrays the people who fail to oppose him as equally unworthy: as venal, corrupt, revolting ... We marvel at the characters Richard III, the Jew of Malta and Flamineo as

essential insights into a savage age. When Brecht provides us with a key
to cataclysmic aspects of our own, we should not dismiss him lightly.

(Needle and Thomson, *Brecht*, Blackwell, 1981)

The play in performance

By putting together notes from those involved in directing
productions of *Arturo Ui* with reviews of key productions, it is
possible to begin to appreciate the theatrical power of the play and
also to realise the many pitfalls that await those attempting to stage
this political parody.

The first production

The world premiere of *Arturo Ui* was at Stuttgart in November
1958, directed by Peter Palitzsch. Manfred Wekwerth, who then
became joint director with Palitzsch of the Berliner Ensemble
production the following year, wrote in his Notes about the first
production:

1. Lessons of a pilot production at another theatre

Scene 1 [1a]

The members of the trust display the same gangsters' attitudes and
costumes as we know from American films; two-tone suits, a variety of
hats, scarves and so on. This misses the point, essential to the story, that
here we have old-established businessmen who have been in the trade
'since Noah's ark'. These trust members are too much like parvenus,
profiteers, so that the element of solid respectability – the bourgeois
element – is lost. As a result their subsequent alliance with Ui, far from
being worthy of remark, seems natural. Gangsters seeking out their own
kind: *not* the bourgeois state turning to something it had expressly
branded as its own mortal enemy – organised crime.

For the same reasons the crisis too is ill-founded, since people who
make such an impression are used to running into money troubles,

because their business (profiteering) involves risks.

Scene 2 [1b]

Ui, Roma, and Ragg emerge on to the apron from below stage and hurry past Clark one by one. In this way they formally announce themselves as gangsters emerging from a sewer manhole and not, as the story demands, as gangsters offering their services to the trust in a particularly offhand and gentleman-like manner.

Scene 3 [2]. Dogsborough's restaurant

Unless Dogsborough appears above all as an immovable, unchangeable, impregnable, rocklike fortress (i.e., solidly or immovably set in an attitude which, to judge from the text, Brecht took from Hindenburg), the great turning point where he crumbles will not be properly brought out. Instead of a 'great personality' succumbing to an economic force we get an average personality doing what is only to be expected. The actor gave us a lively, forceful, decisive, far too young Dogsborough, with an agile mind and agile gestures. When he looked out of the window and succumbed to the house by the lake, he turned round at least two times in order to express his reservations, and in so doing destroyed the great instant of succumbing.

Similarly with Dogsborough's treatment by the trust people. They should not address him as if he were one of their own sort – i.e., in business jargon – but ought to deploy considerable human resources in order to get him to listen to them at all. They should all the time be confirming his reputation as honest old Dogsborough.

As to the identification of the characters with the Nazi leaders: Dogsborough bore no kind of resemblance to Hindenburg, neither of attitude, gesture, tone of voice, nor mask. The necessary degree of likeness to Hindenburg could only be achieved once one had taken in the inscriptions, and after the play had ended. The highly amusing way in which the course of the action instantly and directly alienates the gangsters into top Nazis was missed, or at any rate seemed vague and inexact.

The play was written against Hitler and the big shots of those times. No general conclusions can be drawn until this story, transposed into terms of the gang world, can be concretely recognised so as to allow people in subsequent times to generalise from concrete knowledge and detect fascist trends. To start off by generalising – i.e., by making the characters identifiable not merely with Hitler and Hindenburg – makes the events less concrete and prevents any true historical generalisation. This is particularly true of our own time, where the historical events are barely remembered and the top Nazis virtually unknown except from photographs. Brecht himself rejects such a discreet approach inasmuch as he uses allusive names (Dogsborough, Giri, Roma, etc.), and calls for prescribed similarities of voice, gesture, and masks. Without this the work degenerates into a *roman à clef*.

Scene 4 [3]. Bookmaker's office

In the bookmaker's office the group of leaders – Ui, Ragg, and Roma – associated with the other gangsters, with the result that their discussions degenerated into everyday conversations instead of being a crucial conversation between leading personalities; for the crisis would hardly be discussed before all and sundry. This was accentuated by the unrelievedly pliable, deflated, rubbery, unassertive attitude of Arturo Ui, who was in no way shown as a boss, but more as a passive plaything among strong men. Presented in such a wretched niggling light, his plans did not emerge as dangerous; what was shown was not so much the large-scale planning of lunacy as the actual lunacy itself. This meant that the Nazis' logical approach – which admittedly developed on a basis of lunacy and lack of logic – was never established, so that every subsequent action seemed more or less accidental and not thought up with a vast expenditure of effort. Hence Nazism emerged as haphazard and individualistic instead of being a system: a system based on lunacy and lack of system.

Puny swindles ought to be mightily pondered underhand actions conceived on a vast scale; instances of thoughtlessness realised by enormous thought.

Ui as a character

Ui was presented as a passive plaything in the hands of strong men (Goebbels, Göring, Papen). He has pathological features which ran unchanged right through the play. All through he gave evidence of exhaustion and lack of enterprise, needing to be prompted and jogged by Givola even during his big speeches. In this way the character was emasculated and the main weight of responsibility shifted to the strong men, but without any explanation why they in particular should be strong.

One of the dangerous things about Hitler was his immensely stubborn logic, a logic based on absence of logic, lack of understanding and half-baked ideas. (Even the concentration camps were no accidental creation, having been planned as early as 1923.) Precisely Hitler's languidness, his indecision, emptiness, feebleness, and freedom from ideas were the source of his usefulness and strength.

The impression given in this production was that Hitler's feebleness and malleability were a liability to the movement, and that given greater energy and intelligence fascism would have proved much easier to put up with, since its shortcomings were here attributed to human weakness [. . .]

The investigation [Scene 5]

The legal process failed to come across. It was impossible to tell who has convened the inquiry, who is being accused, what part is being played by Dogsborough, how far an appearance of justice still matters, what official standing Ui has there. This scene accordingly came across as a muddle, not as a bourgeois legal ritual that gangsters can use unchanged. Rituals and arrangements should therefore be portrayed with especial precision and care. Only the dignity of the traditional procedures can show the indignity of what is taking place.

The Warehouse Fire Trial [Scene 8]

This scene was not helped by the symbolic grouping which had the populace represented by Nazis who stood a few inches behind the centrally placed judges (pointing a pistol at their heads!).

The fact that the Nazis needed the seal of approval of the bourgeois court, along with its dignity and traditions, was thereby made incomprehensible. Instead it became an unceremonious gang tribunal, and accordingly without any meaning as a court.

If all that is to appear is how the court's bourgeois traditions are flouted, then it becomes impossible to show how the bourgeois court, by the mere fact of its existence, flouts justice; how crime is an integral part of its traditional procedures; and how it is unnecessary for this tradition to be broken to make it criminal.

(Wekwerth, *Schriften, Arbeit mit Brecht*, East Berlin, Henschel-Verlag, 1973, pp. 144–7)

The Berliner Ensemble production, 1959

This is regarded by most critics as the 'definitive' production of the play, directed by Wekwerth and Palitzsch, with Brecht's son-in-law, Ekkehard Schall as Ui. In his notes about the production, Wekwerth drew attention to one of the problems which has bedevilled all directors and actors working on the play:

After the third rehearsal we gave up trying to base the principal parts on their correspondences with the Nazi originals. The mistake became particularly evident in the case of Schall, who gave an extremely well-observed imitation of Hitler's vocal characteristics and gestures, such as we had seen a day or two before on film. The faithfulness of this imitation wholly swamped the story of the gangster play. What resulted was a highly amusing parody, but of details from a play about Nazis. The more profoundly amusing point – the parallel between Nazis and gangsters – was lost, since it can only be made if the gangster story is sufficiently complete and independent to match the Nazi story. It is the distancing of the one story from the other that allows them to be connected up on a historical-philosophical, not a merely mechanical plane. We asked the actors to be guided by a strong sense of fun, free from all historical ideas, in exploiting their extensive knowledge of American gangster movies, then carefully on top of that to put recognisable quotations from the vocal characteristics and gestures of the Nazi originals, rather as one puts on a mask.

(ibid., pp. 147–8)

John Willett saw this production at the Paris International Theatre Season in 1960. His notes on his impressions of the performance create a clear sense of the impact and excitement of the event as well as the potential of the play in its effect on an audience. Willett writes:

I have just come back from seeing one of the most extraordinary performances in the history of the Paris international theatre festival: Ekkehard Schall playing Arturo Ui. This Ui, a caricatured, parodied, yet always frightening fusion of Hitler and Al Capone (with a dash of Richard III), is the central figure of a blank-verse play which Brecht wrote in a few weeks in 1941. Schall is a young actor whom he appointed to the Berliner Ensemble shortly before his death; we have seen him in London as a violent, yet mannered Eilif in *Mother Courage* and as an over-stylised ADC in *The Caucasian Chalk Circle*. He is certainly not dull, but his acting has often seemed too tense and at the same time contrived; too reminiscent of the Japanese film and the methodical violence of Brando and Dean, and, behind that, of the disciplined horrors of the Third Reich.

One might well wonder what this actor would make of this particular part. For although *The Resistible Rise of Arturo Ui* (to give it its full title) is a play of great verve, in its mock-Elizabethan way, it is by no means one of Brecht's masterpieces, and it seems trivial beside the monstrous realities which it is supposed to reflect. The author was cocking a snook at the Nazis, rather as Chaplin did in *The Great Dictator*, at a time when half Europe was fighting for its life and monsters like Himmler, Kaltenbrunner and Eichmann were making the street-fighting and the concentration camps of the 1930s look like a

Sunday School outing. Because he was satirising Hitler's rise to power, from 1932 to the annexation of Austria, his satire was already out of date. It would surely be very wide of any mark today.

And yet at the Théâtre Sarah Bernhardt both actor and play were uproariously justified. Two of Brecht's East German pupils, Peter Palitzsch and Manfred Wekwerth, in a big, raw, rowdy production, have turned this Chicago allegory from a superficially shallow parody of Nazism into a forceful commentary on the present cult of violence. The setting, the atmosphere, the ear-splitting music are all drawn from the pin-table saloon and the juke box; debased tunes looted from Liszt or Chopin (specified in Brecht's text) boom out over the loudspeakers; naked electric light bulbs frame the stage, like in a fair; peals of happy gangster laughter fill the blackouts in the central trial scene (with its obvious references to the Reichstag Fire) as justice is crudely mocked and fooled. The machine-guns rattle; the gangsters slouch across the blood-spattered revolving stage; and you no longer feel, as the author originally intended, that the Nazis were just petty criminals, blown up to huge proportions by the gale of history. Instead you begin to feel scared that our current brand of senseless brutality could produce such genuine monsters once more.

Against this background we have Schall at first sitting staring and silent in a corner of the stage. Here is something very rare: an actor who can be a great clown, and at the same time a blood-curdling maniac; who can make the audience howl with laughter without forgetting or under-estimating the horrors in which he is taking part. There he slumps, a moody unsuccessful petty gang-leader on the verge of ruin, dressed in a mackintosh and a dirty soft hat, with ghastly red-ringed eyes, ginger hair and a nailbrush moustache. He is truly a pathetic figure as he appeals to the avuncular but corrupt mayor (i.e. Hindenburg) to save him from the police; it seems like some pitiable form of madness as he mutters and grovels and blurts. Then the threats begin – blackmail, offers of 'protection', spoken demagogically over a growling accompaniment on the brass, with sudden unpredictable switches back into a whining or normally conversational tone. The first murders quickly follow: his first short, bloody, but still half-ridiculous appearance in public affairs.

It is a gradual crescendo. The loudspeakers blare; the stage rotates; and Ui stands there in a dinner-jacket, taking a necessary lesson in deportment and declamation from a broken-down Shakespearean actor. Staggering with his head thrown back, pawing the air for a handhold, he learns to walk in the heroic style; to clasp his hands in front of himself, as if caught without trousers; imperiously, if still ineptly, to fold his arms. He practises such motions in front of the mirror, discussing them coldly with the old actor and the cynical slit-mouthed henchman who represents Goebbels; a short burst of tommy-gun fire punctuates his remarks. Then, clumsily following the actor at first, imitating his tones and trying to copy his gestures with one hand as he holds his Shakespeare in the other and squints down at it, he declaims 'Friends, Roman, countrymen . . .' with a mounting conviction which verges on hysteria, dropping back to the ridiculous now and again as he stumbles on a word like 'Lupercal', or strains, like his fellow-ham, to squeeze an authentic tear for 'Caesar hath wept'. It seems like a brilliant (and brilliantly written) 'turn', but even as the audience is applauding the stage spins round again; the Liszt theme roars out; and there is Ui speaking to the crowd, yelling 'Murder! Butchery! Blackmail! Violence! Rape!' through a brassy amplifier, promising 'protection' against these self-invented disorders, and rasping an offer of 'peace and quiet and safety'. He is applying, with occasional comic uncertainty, the lesson and even the gestures which he has just learnt.

One cannot remember or describe it all. There is Ui again, in his hotel room after the trial, cursing and cajoling his lieutenants as they quarrel, cowering as they come to blows, imploring their confidence – their 'Glaube' or faith – in a series of hysterical gulps. Guns are drawn; the furniture bounces and clatters across the stage; there is a half-hypnotised, wholly mawkish reconciliation; and Ui is left alone to rehearse his next speech. 'Friends', he begins, as he clasps his hands in virginal modesty. He moves back a few paces, and begins again ... No good. Back further, up a long carpet to a square, ugly modernistic and unusually springy armchair. He sits in it. 'Friends! ...' He stands up in it. He straddles on top of it, but finds the position too precarious, and steps gingerly down on to the seat again. 'Friends!', he cries. 'With sorrow I have learnt/That treacherously, behind my back ...' and at this point somersaults backwards, in an apparent loss of balance, and disappears suddenly behind the chair.

Fresh start. He gets as far as 'behind my back', then peers cautiously behind him over the chair in each direction, as if defying the same dark forces to pull him over again. He holds his ground and goes on. Some of those closest to him, he shouts, have plotted to betray him. They are hand in glove with big business. 'No, that won't do,' he mutters, and drops down promptly into the attitude of Rodin's Thinker. 'I've got it: hand in glove with the Police!' And he bounces excitedly up and down in the chair, working himself into a rhetorical frenzy until an interruption makes him quickly curl up, very small indeed, between its padded arms.

The murder of Hitler's lieutenant Röhm, to which all this is leading, is paralleled in a scene that might have come from one of the classic gangster films: the melancholy gunmen in oilskins, waiting behind an armour-plated garage door that grinds and whirrs convincingly as it is raised or lowered. Steady rain; nerves and nostalgia, broken by the first loudspeaker warnings from an outpost. 'Police car down Church Street ... moving on.' 'Two cars coming round the corner without lights.' The two cars contain Ui and others of the gang, who in the best Shakespearean tradition butcher all those present, so that the bloodstained stage can spin on to its next scene: a parody of the garden scene in *Faust*, where Ui, now sedate in top hat and tails, and his faithful Goebbels walk peacefully round a flower shop (well stocked with wreaths), talking in rhyming couplets with Mr and Mrs Dullfeet, whom Ui is about to treat as Hitler did Austria on the eve of the war.

Next, inevitably, Dullfeet's (or Dollfuss's) funeral, black and solemn as some painting of the 1860s, as the hypocritical mourners wind past in silence, shaking and furling their umbrellas before entering the church. And then the final triumphal public meeting, where Ui harangues the cowed citizenry from a rostrum with all the methods and madness of the mature Hitler, the surviving businessmen supporting him, and on either side, diagonally across the stage, the gangsters lounging with their guns.

The epilogue, delivered quietly by Schall in front of the curtain, as the applause suddenly snaps off:

Learn how to face the facts you tried to shun
And how to act, where once you idly slept.
That's how the world was going to be run!
The nations duly mastered it, except
(In case you think the battle has been won) –
The womb is fertile still from which that crept.

Garish, strident, savage, the play is over and a stunned audience is left to cheer and perhaps to think. Full marks to the producers, and for Appen's setting and Hosalla's music. Full marks for Schall's marvellously controlled virtuosity. A special cheer for a company whose younger members can carry on a great tradition with such freshness and force, and can incidentally recruit such a very remarkable newcomer as Hilmar Thate, who takes the Goebbels part. A wish that this may help to revitalise our way of staging the Elizabethans. A new respect for Brecht's less good plays. A hope that this production will be seen in London next year.

(Willett, *Brecht in Context*, pp. 251–5)

The production indeed came to London, and was greeted with great acclaim, as part of the Berliner Ensemble's second visit during August 1965. There were, however, critics who drew attention to the difference between play and production, for example Martin Esslin in *Plays and Players*, reviewing the three-week season at the Old Vic Theatre, wrote:

> *The Resistible Rise of Arturo Ui* which aroused the greatest admiration
> on the part of the London critics ... is a weak play made into a success
> by spectacular, virtuoso production.

In this original virtuoso production, the play took place 'in a circus
tent behind a gaily illuminated proscenium' (*The Times*, 10.8.1965).
Before the play opened, the stage was bare except for four
glass cabinets containing life-size dummies of Hindenburg, Hitler,
Göring and Goebbels. The proscenium arch was surrounded with
the coloured lights of a fairground which flashed on and off as the
play opened with a cacophonous blare of loud, vulgar music. As
the four principals were introduced they emerged from behind the
cabinets – building up to a climax which collapsed into bathos with
the appearance of a pathetic little man in a trilby and raincoat.
From then on, each scene was played within a tightly lit area of a
revolving stage, with the next scene being constructed behind it.
The naturalistic detail of each scene was assiduously precise from a
tray of dirty coffee cups in the first scene to the reproduction of
the exact period and style of Dogsborough's house by the lake.
The grouping and lighting of the trial scene occupied a larger area
of the stage. The attention to detail – for example, the press and
witness stands were exact replicas of period equivalents, the robes
of the prosecuting and defending counsel were precise copies –
heightened the farcical nature of the proceedings.

Wekwerth's notes about the music in the production clarify its
impact in the theatre:

> The basic character of the music was dictated by setting the 'great
> historical gangster play' of the prologue within the colourful shooting-
> gallery framework of a fairground. At the same time it was the music's
> job to stress the atmosphere of horror. It had to be garish and nasty.
>
> This suggested the use of pieces of music abused by the Nazis, e.g.,
> the theme from Liszt's *Les Preludes* which they degraded into a
> signature tune for special announcements on the radio. The idea of

playing Chopin's 'Funeral March' at set intervals throughout the long-drawn-out warehouse fire trial was suggested by Brecht. Tempi and rhythms of these themes were of course radically altered to accord with the basic character established for the production.

The orchestra consisted of just a few instruments: trumpet, trombone, tuba, horn, piccolo, clarinet, electric guitar, saxophone, piano, harmonium and percussion.

The sharpness and the fairground effect were furthered by technical effects in the course of recording on tape.

All music was on tape. For the first time the accompaniments to the three songs – Ted Ragg's song poking fun at the delay, Greenwool's soppy 'Home Song' and Givola's 'Whitewash Song' – were all reproduced from tape.

(Wekwerth, *Schriften, Arbeit mit Brecht*, p. 150)

Later productions

The emphasis on the actor's performance as Ui is a marked feature of reviews of successive productions. There are four notable British productions which are well recorded: in 1969 with Leonard Rossiter, in 1978 with Simon Callow, in 1987 with Griff Rhys Jones and in 1991 with Antony Sher. There was also a 1972 television adaptation entitled *The Gangster Show* (directed by Jack Gold with Nicol Williamson as Ui). The most talked about – still – is the production starring Leonard Rossiter, directed by Michael Blakemore. Michael Billington, theatre critic for the *Guardian* newspaper, has described Rossiter's performance in some detail:

The essence of the performance was contained in the first entrance: Rossiter's Ui sprang dramatically through a paper screen like a clown at the start of a circus, spoiling the effect only through the fact that he left a mass of brown paper clinging obstinately to his mouth. From that instant we knew we were in the presence of a man who could never live up to his own mental image of himself, a man for whom there was always a fatal gap between the imaginative intention and the end product. Physically, he was grotesque: the vast-brimmed, top-heavy felt hat made him look like a walking advertisement for Spanish sherry; the wide, board-stiff shoulders suggested a coat from which the hanger had, uncharitably, not been removed; the ungainly, outsize feet splayed out like a pigeon's and had to be picked up whenever he moved as if lead weights were attached to the soles. His walk was a trudge through a ploughed field after heavy rain. But there was also danger and venom behind the grotesquerie. Asked to leave a restaurant by a pin-striped capitalist, he emitted a steam-iron hiss, his head spiralled up like that of a cobra about to strike and then, exercising an iron control, he contented himself with raising his hat in exaggerated mock-politeness. His corkscrew body constantly seemed to be in the grip of some barely restrainable animal force but, at the same time, the absurdity balanced the menace: resting his finger delicately on a chair-back, he let forth a pig-like squeal of pain when someone actually sat down on the chair.

To make evil funny is a singular achievement; and this is precisely what Rossiter did. And nowhere was the technique of balancing the laughter and the absurdity better demonstrated than in the classic scene where Ui is given lessons in deportment and declamation by a veteran Shakespearean actor. The actor firstly showed him how to enter a room, flinging his right arm over his left shoulder as if wrapping a cloak about himself: Ui imitated this with passable effectiveness. He was told to walk on the points of his shoes: he dutifully did so, shooting out his legs like a demented chorine until we saw the evolution of the goose-step. Instructed to stand with his hands neutrally folded in front of him, he seized his crotch with rabid intensity and shot white-toothed, manic smiles at his colleagues as if seeking approbation. Taught to speak with theatrical clarity, his tongue stumbled over the word 'hath' and then flicked out like a lizard's as he tried to master the insuperably difficult verb. Movement and speech thus mastered, next came the art of sitting with the legs placed wide apart and the hands planted firmly on the thighs. From this position he essayed a multi-purpose, Roman-history-play gesture of authority; gradually he realised it was more impressive if the arm was stiff and unbent; and with a gleaming, and delirious self-approval, he achieved the first-ever Nazi salute. Thus the most remarkable transformation-scene in the whole of modern drama took place. [. . .] A great performance. Partly because of its sheer mimetic vitality; partly because it left behind an ineradicable physical image as of an animated Grosz cartoon; partly because of its truth to the Brechtian ideal in that it revealed the abject cowardice and fear behind the character's public mask of brutality. 'The actor,' wrote Brecht, 'must make himself observed standing *between* the spectator and the text.' And in the most imaginative and potent way possible that is precisely what Rossiter did.

(Billington, *The Modern Actor*, Hamish Hamilton, 1973, pp. 72–4)

A triumph for Rossiter, then, but the Brechtian device of caption titles linking the action of the play to history was dropped, the director, Michael Blakemore opting to rely on the power of the mimetic acting to generate the necessary historical links in the minds of the audience. Similarly but more extensively (as detailed in an article by Pete Mathers in *Screen*, Winter 1995/6, vol. 16, no. 4), Jack Gold, in creating *The Gangster Show* for the BBC TV series Play of the Month, adapted the play for the audience of a different medium. Not only were there no historical titles, he also cut large sections of the Prologue and early scenes, throwing the focus more quickly on to the character of Ui with little by way of introduction to the members of the Cauliflower Trust. He also changed the nature of the relationship between Ui's three lieutenants, reducing their roles from those evident in the play. The film was shot on location in England in a style which emphasised close-ups of characters. However Nicol Williamson's portrayal of Ui was received warmly.

In the 1978 production at the Half Moon Theatre in East London, Robert Walker directed Simon Callow as Ui. A critic at the time, Geoff Brown, writing in *Plays*, gave details of Callow's well-received interpretation:

> Brecht manipulates this common fund of knowledge to provide a
> ferocious, mocking portrait of an idiot dictator idiotically given power.
> And the Arturo Ui of the excellent Simon Callow is an equally
> ferocious creation, maniacally glowering with a false nose and a token
> black moustache hanging from the nostrils. He begins his first scene
> squatting, silent and still, under the metal-slatted platform which
> provides the main acting area: he seems almost made out of putty,
> squeezed into a series of monstrously grotesque postures round the
> bare-boned set. In his speech, he seems half Chico Marx, half gorilla.
> But once he receives lessons in posture and dramatic recitation from a
> has-been actor (as Hitler did), he becomes more ridiculous than ever –
> accompanying his rantings with the thrusts of clenched fists, outflung
> fingers and thumps on the thigh. It's a fantastic performance ...

In his *Guardian* review of the 1987 production (directed by David
Gilmore at the Queens Theatre, London, with Griff Rhys Jones as
Ui), Michael Billington underlines what had come to be seen as a
central irony of the play:

> One of the supreme Brechtian ironies is that the supposed master of
> ensemble wrote some of the fattest star-parts in the modern repertory.
> And star-roles don't come much fatter than the gangster-hero of Arturo
> Ui whom twenty years ago Leonard Rossiter turned into an
> unforgettable figure of galvanic absurdity and whom Simon Callow in
> 1978 at the Half Moon played as a memorable lank-locked, false-nosed
> grotesque.

Reviews of the central performance – and hence the success of the
production – were mixed. Whereas the *Daily Mirror* critic, David
Nathan, felt that 'Griff Rhys Jones chillingly portrays the
mediocrity of the Nazi who won power by a combination of his
own savagery and the greed and cowardice of the businessmen who
thought they could control him', Andrew Rissik, writing in the

Independent, judged:

> To begin with, Griff Rhys Jones's Arturo Ui is a brilliant display of
> mimetic caricature, hyperactive and button-eyed, like a sinister Charlie
> Chaplin, but when he speaks we get stuck with a rasping warm-up man.
> This Arturo moves like a psychopath, nervously agile, itching with
> tentative viciousness and skittishly self-satisfied. But his voice is hoarse
> and opaque, and too often the lines are delivered in a near-falsetto
> gabble, so that our imagination flinches at the idea that this craven
> buffoon could ever have commanded the loyalty of Givola or Roma or
> Linal Haft's swaggeringly odious Giri. What we are watching is
> something closer to Chaplin's *The Great Dictator* than the venomous
> polemical satire of Brecht's play, something nearer practical joke than
> political cartoon. This Arturo cannot yet darken the stage so that our
> laughter freezes as he speaks.

This production did retain the projected titles, as is evident from
Giles Gordon's condemnatory review for the London *Daily News*:

> And just in case we somehow miss the parallels with the 1930s rise of
> the Nazis, Brecht, not a subtle man, tells the entire plot in a prologue
> and projects sentences on a screen before each scene so that we know
> what is going to happen. Alienation is indeed achieved.

It was not until 1991 that a further major production of *Arturo
Ui* was seen in London, this time at the National Theatre, directed
by Di Trevis and starring Antony Sher. Sher's performance
received rave reviews; the actor's virtuosity being highly praised. In
what the Marxist critic, Terry Eagleton, in the *Times Literary
Supplement*, described as a 'Brechtian extravaganza, packing in
everything from tap-dance routines to a real motor car', Sher
created his version of Ui:

> Like his predecessors in the role, he starts by inscribing a static image of
> the monster before setting it in motion: Sher's image being that of an
> abject sewer rat hovering at the tables of the rich with burning eyes.

> Then comes the avalanche of detail. At a reference to Richard III, his
> two sub-machine-guns turn into crutches. Goaded by a reporter, he
> casually beats him up while presenting himself as the victim. Launching
> a volley of threats against Dogsborough (Hindenburg) he gets hopelessly
> entangled in the old man's deckchair, which redoubles his wrath and
> carries him on to victory. Humiliation for him is a source of power.
> The basic idea of the performance is simple: the aggressor as underdog.
>
> (Irving Wardle, *Independent on Sunday*)

However, Wardle also draws attention to the problems posed by
the style of the production, a more difficult concept to discover
from the reviews of the production.

> More damaging is the show's presentational style. *Arturo Ui* was written
> as an allegory in a popular American form. Trevis and team have given
> it the Piscator treatment. The immediate impact is extremely impressive,
> thanks largely to Nick Holder in the interpolated role of the gangland
> MC, whose translation of Brechtian captions into ringingly sinister
> recitative sends shivers down the spine. But whenever the music, the
> screen projections, and other magnifying devices shut down, the acting
> looks small.

Throughout Europe the play has been produced to demonstrate the
ongoing relevance of Brecht's central message. In the Warsaw
production of 1962 Tadeusz Lomnicki tried a different tack in
interpreting the role of Ui. According to Jan Kott in his *Theatre
Notebook* (Methuen, 1968, p. 106), Lomnicki started physically and
vocally quite unrecognisable as the historical Hitler:

> In the first scene Lomnicki is hanging over a balustrade. He is all
> flabby, like a punctured balloon. He turns round; he is small, plain, soft
> – nothing much to look at with his triangular powdered face and beetle
> brows ... It is the face of a clown with the red line of the mouth, the
> goggling eyes.

But gradually the actor took on the familiar cartoon characteristics as Ui begins to realise his potential:

> The jerky clown grows in stature and suddenly becomes Hitler. Even in
> the first scene he was never funny but now he is frightening. He still
> has the face of the clown and ridiculous beetle brows. He has not ceased
> to be a clown, but he has also become Hitler; he has adopted Hitler's
> gestures and is setting the world on fire.

There have also been attempts to update the topicality of Ui. For
example, in 1987 Alfred Kirchner directed a production at the
Vienna Burgtheater in which the gangsters wore loden coats and
Tyrolean hats in reference to the contemporary controversy
centring on the Austrian Chancellor Kurt Waldheim's supposed
Nazi involvement.

Brecht's writings about *Arturo Ui*

Brecht gave some precise instructions as to how the play should be
performed.

Instructions for performance
In order that the events may retain the significance unhappily due
them, the play must be performed in the grand style, and preferably
with obvious harkbacks to the Elizabethan theatre, i.e., with curtains and
different levels. For instance, the action could take place in front of
curtains of whitewashed sacking spattered the colour of ox blood. At
some points panorama-like backdrops could be used, and organ, trumpet
and drum effects are likewise permissible. Use should be made of the
masks, vocal characteristics, and gestures of the originals; pure parody
however must be avoided, and the comic element must not preclude
horror. What is needed is a three-dimensional presentation which goes at
top speed and is composed of clearly defined groupings like those
favoured by historical tableaux at fairs.

('Hinweis für die Aufführung', from GW *Stücke*, pp. 1837–8)

Brecht also left other writings which deal with aspects of the play and his intentions in writing it.

Notes

1. Preface

The Resistible Rise of Arturo Ui, written in Finland in 1941, represents an attempt to make Hitler's rise intelligible to the capitalist world by transposing that rise into a sphere thoroughly familiar to it. The blank verse is an aid in appraising the characters' heroism.

2. Remarks

Nowadays ridiculing the great political criminals, alive or dead, is generally said to be neither appropriate or constructive. Even the common people are said to be sensitive on this point, not just because they too were implicated in the crimes in question but because it is not possible for those who survived among the ruins to laugh about such things. Nor is it much good hammering at open doors (as there are too many of these among the ruins anyway): the lesson has been learned, so why go on dinning it into the poor creatures? If on the other hand the lesson has not been learned it is risky to encourage people to laugh at a potentate after once failing to take him seriously enough; and so on and so forth.

It is relatively easy to dismiss the suggestion that art needs to treat brutality with kid gloves; that it should devote itself to watering the puny seedlings of awareness; that it ought to be explaining the garden hose to former wielders of the rubber truncheon, and so on. Likewise it is possible to object to the term 'people', as used to signify something 'higher' than population, and to show how the term conjures up the notorious concept of *Volksgemeinschaft*, or a 'sense of being one people,' that links executioner and victim, employer and employed. But this does not mean that the suggestion that satire should not meddle in serious matters is an acceptable one. Serious things are its specific concern.

The great political criminals must be completely stripped bare and exposed to ridicule. Because they are not great political criminals at all, but the perpetrators of great political crimes, which is something very different.

There is no need to be afraid of truisms so long as they are true. If the collapse of Hitler's enterprises is no evidence that he was a halfwit, neither is their scale any guarantee that he was a great man. In the main the classes that control the modern state use utterly average people for their enterprises. Not even in the highly important field of economic exploitation is any particular talent called for. A multimillion-Mark trust like I.G. Farben makes use of exceptional intelligence only when it can exploit it; the exploiters proper, a handful of people most of whom acquired their power by birth, have a certain cunning and brutality as a group but see no commercial drawbacks in lack of education, nor even in the presence among them of the odd amiable individual. They get their political affairs dealt with by people often markedly stupider than themselves. Thus Hitler was no doubt a lot more stupid than Brünning, and Brünning than Stresemann, while on the military plane Keitel and Hindenburg were much of a muchness. A military specialist like Ludendorff, who lost battles by his political immaturity, is no more to be thought of as an intellectual giant than is someone who performs feats of lightning mathematical calculation from the music-hall. It is the scope of their enterprises that gives such people their aura of greatness. But this aura does not necessarily make them all that effective, since it only means that there is a vast mass of intelligent people available, with the result that wars and crises become displays of the intelligence of the entire population.

On top of that it is a fact that crime itself frequently provokes admiration. I never heard the petty bourgeoisie of my home town speak with anything but respectful enthusiasm of a man called Kneisel who was a mass murderer, with the result that I have remembered his name to this day. It was not even thought necessary on his behalf to invent the usual acts of kindness towards poor old grannies: his murders were enough.

In the main the petty bourgeois conception of history (and the

proletariat's too, so long as it has no other), is a romantic one. What
fired these Germans' poverty-stricken imagination in the case of
Napoleon I was of course not his Code Napoléon but his millions of
victims. Bloodstains embellish these conquerors' faces like beauty spots.
When a certain Dr Pechel, writing in the aptly named *Deutsche
Rundschau* in 1946, said of Genghis Khan that 'the price of the Pax
Mongolica was the death of several dozen million men and the
destruction of twenty kingdoms', it made a great man of this
'bloodstained conqueror, the demolisher of all values, though this must
not cause us to forget the ruler who showed that his real nature was not
destructive' – on the mere grounds that he was never small in his
dealings with people. It is this reverence for killers that has to be done
away with. Plain everyday logic must never let itself be overawed once
it goes strolling among the centuries; whatever applies to small situations
must be made to apply to big ones too. The petty rogue whom the
rulers permit to become a rogue on the grand scale can occupy a special
position in roguery, but not in our attitude to history. Anyway there is
truth in the principle that comedy is less likely than tragedy to omit to
take human suffering seriously enough.

Brecht also wrote notes countering some of the criticisms that had
been levelled at the play by other German writers.

3. Jottings

Kusche: '. . . but at the very point where the projections unmistakably
relate *Ui* to a specific phase of German history . . . the question arises:
"Where is the People?"

'Brecht has written, apropos of Eisler's *Faustus*, that "our starting
point has to be the truth of the phrase 'no conception can be valid that
assumes German history to be unalloyed *misère* and fails to present the
People as a creative force' ".

'What is lacking is something or other that would stand for this
"creative force of the People" . . . Was it all a mere internal affray
between gangsters and merchants? Was Dimitroff (as it is simpler to give
that force an individual name) a merchant?'

Ui is a *parable* play, written with the aim of destroying the dangerous respect commonly felt for great killers. The circle described has been deliberately restricted; it is confined to the plane of state, industrialists, Junkers and petty bourgeois. This is enough to achieve the desired objective. The play does not pretend to give a complete account of the historical situation in the 1930s. The proletariat is not present, nor could it be taken into account more than it is, since anything *extra* in this complex would be *too much*; it would distract from the tricky problem posed. (How could more attention be paid to the proletariat without considering unemployment, and how could that be done without dealing with the [Nazi] employment programme, likewise with the political parties and their abdication? One thing would entail another, and the result would be a gigantic work which would fail to do what was intended.)

The projected texts [signs] – which K. takes as a reason for expecting the play to give a general account of what happened – seem to me, if anything, to stress the element of selectivity, of a peep-show.

The industrialists all seem to have been hit by the crisis to the same extent, whereas the stronger ought to knock out the weaker. (But that may be another point which would involve us in too much detail and which a *parable* can legitimately skip.) The Defence Counsel in the warehouse fire trial, possibly needs another look. At present his protests seem designed merely to defend a kind of 'honour of the profession'. The audience will of course want to see him as Dimitroff, whether it was meant to or not.

As for the appearance of Röhm's ghost, I think Kusche is right. ('As the text now stands it makes a drunken Nazi slob look like a martyr.') [. . .]

The play was written in 1941 and conceived as a 1941 production.

(GW *Schriften zum Theater*, pp. 1176–80)

Further Reading

Bertolt Brecht: *Brecht on Theatre* (translation and notes by John Willett), Methuen, London, 1964; second edition, 1974. Brecht's essential theoretical and critical writings assembled in one handy volume.

Graham Bartram and Anthony Waine: *Brecht in Perspective*, Longman, London and New York, 1982. Essays by British scholars which examine Brecht's literary, historical and social background, relate him to the German theatrical tradition, and compare him with seminal figures like Piscator and Stanislavsky.

Keith A. Dickson: *Towards Utopia*, Oxford University Press, 1978. Closely argued study of Brecht and his work which draws on research in English, German and Russian. Dickson pursues the utopian vision behind Brecht's satirical presentation of life. The book is organised around themes (Man and Society, the Historical Perspective, etc.) and deals with plays, poetry and prose.

Martin Esslin: *Brecht: a Choice of Evils*, Methuen, London, 1984. An early appraisal with useful insights, in spite of the writer's obvious antipathy to Brecht's politics.

Claude Hill: *Bertolt Brecht*, Twayne, Boston, 1975. An American survey, clear and useful, with separate chapters on major works.

James K. Lyon: *Bertolt Brecht in America*, Methuen, London, 1982. Fascinating account of Brecht's US exile.

Michael Morley: *Brecht, a Study*, Heinemann, London, 1977. A succinct survey of Brecht's work, including the poems, with the plays grouped in chapters according to theme or style.

Jan Needle and Peter Thomson: *Brecht*, Blackwell, Oxford, 1981. The authors have studied Brecht in English translation. They are best on the plays in performance.

Peter Thomson and Glendyr Sacks: *The Cambridge Companion to Brecht*, Cambridge University Press, 1994. A useful general background.

Klaus Völker: *Brecht Chronicle*, Seabury Press, New York, 1975. Detailed biography relating events in Brecht's personal, artistic and political life to his own letters and other writings.

Alfred D. White: *Bertolt Brecht's Great Plays*, Macmillan, London, 1978. Analyses of the major plays in separate chapters.

John Willett: *The Theatre of Bertolt Brecht*, 4th ed., Methuen, London, 1977. Seminal compendium of basic information.

John Willett: *Brecht in Context*, Methuen, London, 1984; revised edition, 1998. Looks at Brecht from several aspects such as politics, music, expressionism etc. Includes Willett's impressions of the Berliner Ensemble production of *Arturo Ui*.

All Brecht's major plays (and many minor works) are published by Methuen Drama in English translation in *Brecht: Collected Plays*, vols 1–8. Also published by Methuen Drama as volumes of Brecht's *Diaries 1920–22*, *Journals 1934–1955* and *Brecht on Art and Politics*. Published by Methuen Publishing Limited Brecht's *Poems 1913–56*, *Short Stories 1921–46* and *Letters 1913–1956*.

The Resistible Rise of Arturo Ui
A parable play

Collaborator: M. STEFFIN

Translator: RALPH MANHEIM

Characters
THE ANNOUNCER
FLAKE ⎫
CARUTHER ⎪ *Businessmen, directors of the*
BUTCHER ⎬ *Cauliflower Trust*
MULBERRY ⎪
CLARK ⎭
SHEET, *shipyard owner*
OLD DOGSBOROUGH
YOUNG DOGSBOROUGH
ARTURO UI, *gang leader*
ERNESTO ROMA, *his lieutenant*
EMANUELE GIRI, *gangster*
The florist GIUSEPPE GIVOLA, *gangster*
TED RAGG, *reporter on* The Star
DOCKDAISY
BOWL, *Sheet's chief accountant*
GOODWILL *and* GAFFLES, *members of the city council*
O'CASEY, *investigator*
AN ACTOR
HOOK, *wholesale vegetable dealer*
DEFENDANT FISH
THE DEFENCE COUNSEL
THE JUDGE
THE DOCTOR
THE PROSECUTOR
A WOMAN
YOUNG INNA, *Roma's familiar*
A LITTLE MAN
IGNATIUS DULLFEET
BETTY DULLFEET, *his wife*
Dogsborough's BUTLER
Bodyguards, Gunmen, Vegetable dealers of Chicago and
Cicero, Reporters

Prologue

The Announcer steps before the curtain. Large notices are attached to the curtain: 'New developments in dock subsidy scandal' ... 'The true facts about Dogsborough's will and confession' ... 'Sensation at warehouse fire trial' ... 'Friends murder gangster Ernesto Roma' ... 'Ignatius Dullfeet blackmailed and murdered' ... 'Cicero taken over by gangsters'. Behind the curtain popular dance music.

THE ANNOUNCER:
    Friends, tonight we're going to show –
    Pipe down, you boys in the back row!
    And, lady, your hat is in the way! –
    Our great historical gangster play
    Containing, for the first time, as you'll see
    The truth about the scandalous dock subsidy.
    Further we give you, for your betterment
    Dogsborough's confession and testament.
    Arturo Ui's rise while the stock market fell.
    The notorious warehouse fire trial. What a sell!
    The Dullfeet murder! Justice in a coma!
    Gang warfare: the killing of Ernesto Roma!
    All culminating in our stunning last tableau:
    Gangsters take over the town of Cicero!
    Brilliant performers will portray
    The most eminent gangsters of our day.
    You'll see some dead and some alive
    Some by-gone and others that survive
    Some born, some made – for instance, here we show

The good old honest Dogsborough!
Old Dogsborough steps before the curtain.
His hair is white, his heart is black.
Corrupt old man, you may step back.
Dogsborough bows and steps back.
The next exhibit on our list
Is Givola –
Givola has stepped before the curtain.
                – the horticulturist.
His tongue's so slippery he'd know how
To sell you a billy-goat for a cow!
Short, says the proverb, are the legs of lies.
Look at his legs, just use your eyes.
Givola steps back limping.
Now to Emanuele Giri, the super-clown.
Come out, let's look you up and down!
Giri steps before the curtain and waves his hand at the audience.
One of the greatest killers ever known!
Okay, beat it!
Giri steps back with an angry look.
And lastly Public Enemy Number One
Arturo Ui. Now you'll see
The biggest gangster of all times
Whom heaven sent us for our crimes
Our weakness and stupidity!
Arturo Ui steps before the curtain and walks out along the footlights.
Doesn't he make you think of Richard the Third?
Has anybody ever heard
Of blood so ghoulishly and lavishly shed
Since wars were fought for roses white and red?
In view of this the management
Has spared no cost in its intent
To picture his spectacularly vile
Manoeuvres in the grandest style.
But everything you'll see tonight is true.

Nothing's invented, nothing's new
Or made to order just for you.
The gangster play that we present
Is known to our whole continent.
While the music swells and the sound of a machine-gun mingles with it, the Announcer retires with an air of bustling self-importance.

I

a

*Financial district. Enter five businessmen, the directors of the
Cauliflower Trust.*

FLAKE: The times are bad.
CLARK: It looks as if Chicago
  The dear old girl, while on her way to market
  Had found her pocket torn and now she's starting
  To scrabble in the gutter for her pennies.
CARUTHER: Last Thursday Jones invited me and eighty
  More to a partridge dinner to be held
  This Monday. If we really went, we'd find
  No one to greet us but the auctioneer.
  This awful change from glut to destitution
  Has come more quickly than a maiden's blush.
  Vegetable fleets with produce for this city
  Still ply the lakes, but nowhere will you find
  A buyer.
BUTCHER: It's like darkness at high noon.
MULBERRY: Robber and Clive are being auctioned off.
CLARK: Wheeler – importing fruit since Noah's ark –
  Is bankrupt.
FLAKE: And Dick Havelock's garages
  Are liquidiating.
CARUTHER: Where is Sheet?
FLAKE: Too busy
  To come. He's dashing round from bank to bank.
CLARK: What? Sheet?
  Pause.

                          In other words, the cauliflower
    Trade in this town is through.
BUTCHER: Come, gentlemen
    Chin up! We're not dead yet.
MULBERRY: Call this a life?
BUTCHER: Why all the gloom? The produce business in
    This town is basically sound. Good times
    And bad, a city of four million needs
    Fresh vegetables. Don't worry. We'll pull through.
CARUTHER: How are the stores and markets doing?
MULBERRY: Badly.
    The customers buy half a head of cabbage
    And that on credit.
CLARK: Our cauliflower's rotting.
FLAKE: Say, there's a fellow waiting in the lobby –
    I only mention it because it's odd –
    The name is Ui . . .
CLARK: The gangster?
FLAKE: Yes, in person.
    He's smelled the stink and thinks he sees an opening.
    Ernesto Roma, his lieutenant, says
    They can convince shopkeepers it's not healthy
    To handle other people's cauliflower.
    He promises our turnover will double
    Because, he says, the shopkeepers would rather
    Buy cauliflower than coffins.
    They laugh dejectedly.
CARUTHER: It's an outrage.
MULBERRY, *laughing uproariously*:
    Bombs and machine guns! New conceptions of
    Salesmanship! That's the ticket. Fresh young
    Blood in the Cauliflower Trust. They heard
    We had insomnia, so Mr Ui
    Hastens to offer us his services.
    Well, fellows, we'll just have to choose. It's him

Or the Salvation Army. Which one's soup
Do you prefer?

CLARK: I tend to think that Ui's
Is hotter.

CARUTHER: Throw him out!

MULBERRY: Politely though.
How do we know what straits we'll come to yet?
They laugh.

FLAKE, *to Butcher*:
What about Dogsborough and a city loan?
To the others.
Butcher and I cooked up a little scheme
To help us through our present money troubles.
I'll give it to you in a nutshell. Why
Shouldn't the city that takes in our taxes
Give us a loan, let's say, for docks that we
Would undertake to build, so vegetables
Can be brought in more cheaply? Dogsborough
Is influential. He could put it through.
Have you seen Dogsborough?

BUTCHER: Yes. He refuses
To touch it.

FLAKE: He refuses? Damn it, he's
The ward boss on the waterfront, and he
Won't help us!

CARUTHER: I've contributed for years
To his campaign fund.

MULBERRY: Hell, he used to run
Sheet's lunchroom. Before he took up politics
He got his bread and butter from the Trust.
That's rank ingratitude. It's just like I've been
Telling you, Flake. All loyalty is gone!
Money is short, but loyalty is shorter.
Cursing, they scurry from the sinking ship
Friend turns to foe, employee snubs his boss
And our old lunchroom operator

Who used to be all smiles is one cold shoulder.
Morals go overboard in times of crisis.

CARUTHER: I'd never have expected that of Dogsborough.

FLAKE: What's his excuse?

BUTCHER: He says our proposition
Is fishy.

FLAKE: What's fishy about building docks?
Think of the men we'd put to work.

BUTCHER: He says
He has his doubts about our building docks.

FLAKE: Outrageous!

BUTCHER: What? Not building?

FLAKE: No. His doubts.

CLARK: Then find somebody else to push the loan.

MULBERRY: Sure, there are other people.

BUTCHER: True enough.
But none like Dogsborough. No, take it easy.
The man is good.

CLARK: For what?

BUTCHER: He's honest. And
What's more, reputed to be honest.

FLAKE: Rot!

BUTCHER: He's got to think about his reputation.
That's obvious.

FLAKE: Who gives a damn? We need
A loan from City Hall. His reputation
Is his affair.

BUTCHER: You think so? I should say
It's ours. It takes an honest man to swing
A loan like this, a man they'd be ashamed
To ask for proofs and guarantees. And such
A man is Dogsborough. Old Dogsborough's
Our loan. All right, I'll tell you why. Because they
Believe in him. They may have stopped believing
In God, but not in Dogsborough. A hard-boiled
Broker, who takes a lawyer with him to

His lawyer's, wouldn't hesitate to put his
Last cent in Dogsborough's apron for safe keeping
If he should see it lying on the bar.
Two hundred pounds of honesty. In eighty
Winters he's shown no weakness. Such a man
Is worth his weight in gold – especially
To people with a scheme for building docks
And building kind of slowly.

FLAKE: Okay, Butcher
He's worth his weight in gold. The deal he vouches
For is tied up. The only trouble is:
He doesn't vouch for ours.

CLARK: Oh no, not he!
'The city treasury is not a grab bag!'

MULBERRY: And 'All for the city, the city for itself!'

CARUTHER: Disgusting. Not an ounce of humour.

MULBERRY: Once
His mind's made up, an earthquake wouldn't change it.
To him the city's not a place of wood
And stone, where people live with people
Struggling to feed themselves and pay the rent
But words on paper, something from the Bible.
The man has always gotten on my nerves.

CLARK: His heart was never with us. What does he care
For cauliflower and the trucking business?
Let every vegetable in the city rot
You think he'd lift a finger? No, for nineteen years
Or is it twenty, we've contributed
To his campaign fund. Well, in all that time
The only cauliflower he's ever seen
Was on his plate. What's more, he's never once
Set foot in a garage.

BUTCHER: That's right.

CLARK: The devil
Take him!

BUTCHER: Oh no! We'll take him.

FLAKE: But Clark says
    It can't be done. The man has turned us down.
BUTCHER: That's so. But Clark has also told us why.
CLARK: The bastard doesn't know which way is up.
BUTCHER: Exactly. What's his trouble? Ignorance.
    He hasn't got the faintest notion what
    It's like to be in such a fix. The question
    Is therefore how to put him in our skin.
    In short, we've got to educate the man.
    I've thought it over. Listen, here's my plan.
    A sign appears, recalling certain incidents in the recent past.*

b

Outside the produce exchange. Flake and Sheet in conversation.

SHEET: I've run from pillar to post. Pillar was out
    Of town, and Post was sitting in the bathtub.
    Old friends show nothing but their backs. A brother
    Buys wilted shoes before he meets his brother
    For fear his brother will touch him for a loan.
    Old partners dread each other so they use
    False names when meeting in a public place.
    Our citizens are sewing up their pockets.
FLAKE: So what about my proposition?
SHEET: No. I
    Won't sell. You want a five-course dinner for the
    Price of the tip. And to be thanked for the tip
    At that. You wouldn't like it if
    I told you what I think of you.
FLAKE: Nobody
    Will pay you any more.

* See the Chronological Table at the end of the play.

SHEET: And friends won't be
  More generous than anybody else.
FLAKE: Money is tight these days.
SHEET: Especially
  For those in need. And who can diagnose
  A friend's need better than a friend?
FLAKE: You'll lose
  Your shipyard either way.
SHEET: And that's not all
  I'll lose. I've got a wife who's likely to
  Walk out on me.
FLAKE: But if you sell . . .
SHEET: . . . she'll last another year. But what I'm curious
  About is why you want my shipyard.
FLAKE: Hasn't
  It crossed your mind that we – I mean the Trust –
  Might want to help you?
SHEET: No, it never crossed
  My mind. How stupid of me to suspect you
  Of trying to grab my property, when you
  Were only trying to help.
FLAKE: Such bitterness
  Dear Sheet, won't save you from the hammer.
SHEET: At least, dear Flake, it doesn't help the hammer.
  Three men saunter past: Arturo Ui, the gangster, his lieutenant
  Ernesto Roma, and a bodyguard. In passing, Ui stares at Flake
  as though expecting to be spoken to, while, in leaving, Roma turns
  his head and gives Flake an angry look.
SHEET: Who's that?
FLAKE: Arturo Ui, the gangster . . . How
  About it? Are you selling?
SHEET: He seemed eager
  To speak to you.
FLAKE, *laughing angrily*: And so he is. He's been
  Pursuing us with offers, wants to sell
  Our cauliflower with his tommy guns.

The town is full of types like that right now
Corroding it like leprosy, devouring
A finger, then an arm and shoulder. No one
Knows where it comes from, but we all suspect
From deepest hell. Kidnapping, murder, threats
Extortion, blackmail, massacre:
'Hands up!' 'Your money or your life!' Outrageous!
It's got to be wiped out.

SHEET, *looking at him sharply*: And quickly. It's contagious.

FLAKE: Well, how about it? Are you selling?

SHEET, *stepping back and looking at him*:
No doubt about it: a resemblance to
Those three who just passed by. Not too pronounced
But somehow there, one senses more than sees it.
Under the water of a pond sometimes
You see a branch, all green and slimy. It
Could be a snake. But no, it's definitely
A branch. Or is it? That's how you resemble
Roma. Don't take offence. But when I looked
At him just now and then at you, it seemed
To me I'd noticed it before, in you
And others, without understanding. Say it
Again, Flake: 'How about it? Are you selling?'
Even your voice, I think . . . No, better say
'Hands up!' because that's what you really mean.
He puts up his hands.
All right, Flake, Take the shipyard!
Give me a kick or two in payment. Hold it!
I'll take the higher offer. Make it two.

FLAKE: You're crazy!

SHEET: I only wish that that were true.

2

Back room in Dogsborough's restaurant. Dogsborough and his son are washing glasses. Enter Butcher and Flake.

DOGSBOROUGH: You didn't need to come. The answer is
  No. Your proposition stinks of rotten fish.
YOUNG DOGSBOROUGH: My father turns it down.
BUTCHER: Forget it, then.
  We ask you. You say no. So no it is.
DOGSBOROUGH: It's fishy. I know your kind of docks.
  I wouldn't touch it.
YOUNG DOGSBOROUGH: My father wouldn't touch it.
BUTCHER: Good.
  Forget it.
DOGSBOROUGH: You're on the wrong road, fellows.
  The city treasury is not a grab bag
  For everyone to dip his fingers into.
  Anyway, damn it all, your business is
  Perfectly sound.
BUTCHER: What did I tell you, Flake?
  You fellows are too pessimistic.
DOGSBOROUGH: Pessimism
  Is treason. You're only making trouble for
  Yourselves. I see it this way: What do you
  Fellows sell? Cauliflower. That's as good
  As meat and bread. Man doesn't live by bread
  And meat alone, he needs his green goods.
  Suppose I served up sirloin without onions
  Or mutton without beans. I'd never see
  My customers again. Some people are
  A little short right now. They hesitate
  To buy a suit. But people have to eat.

They'll always have a dime for vegetables.
Chin up! If I were you, I wouldn't worry.
FLAKE: It does me good to hear you, Dogsborough.
It gives a fellow courage to go on.
BUTCHER: Dogsborough, it almost makes me laugh to find
You so staunchly confident about the future
Of cauliflower, because quite frankly we
Have come here for a purpose. No, don't worry.
Not what you think, that's dead and buried. Something
Pleasant, or so at least we hope. Old man
It's come to our attention that it's been
Exactly twenty-three years this June, since you –
Well known to us for having operated
The lunchroom in one of our establishments for
More than three decades – left us to devote
Your talents to the welfare of this city.
Yes, without you our town would not be what
It is today. Nor, like the city, would
The Trust have prospered as it has. I'm glad
To hear you call it sound, for yesterday
Moved by this festive occasion, we resolved
In token of our high esteem, as proof
That in our hearts we somehow still regard you
As one of us, to offer you the major share
Of stock in Sheet's shipyard for twenty thousand
Dollars, or less than half its value.
He lays the packet of stocks on the bar.
DOGSBOROUGH: I
Don't understand.
BUTCHER: Quite frankly, Dogsborough
The Cauliflower Trust is not reputed
For tenderness of heart, but yesterday
After we'd made our . . . well, our
Stupid request about the loan, and heard
Your answer, honest, incorruptible
Old Dogsborough to a hair, a few of us –

It's not an easy thing to say – were close
To tears. Yes, one man said – don't interrupt
Me, Flake, I won't say who – 'Good God'
He said, 'the man has saved us from ourselves.'
For some time none of us could speak. Then this
Suggestion popped up of its own accord.

DOGSBOROUGH:
I've heard you, friends. But what is there behind it?

BUTCHER: What should there be behind it? It's an offer.

FLAKE: And one that we are really pleased to make.
For here you stand behind your bar, a tower
Of strength, a sterling name, the model of
An upright citizen. We find you washing
Glasses, but you have cleansed our souls as well.
And yet you're poorer than your poorest guest.
It wrings our hearts.

DOGSBOROUGH: I don't know what to say.

BUTCHER: Don't say a word. Just take this little package.
An honest man can use it, don't you think?
By golly, it's not often that the gravy train
Travels the straight and narrow. Take your boy here:
I know a good name's better than a bank
Account, and yet I'm sure he won't despise it.
Just take the stuff and let us hope you won't
Read us the riot act for *this*!

DOGSBOROUGH: Sheet's shipyard!

FLAKE: Look, you can see it from right here.

DOGSBOROUGH, *at the window*:   I've seen it
For twenty years.

FLAKE: We thought of that.

DOGSBOROUGH: And what is
Sheet going to do?

FLAKE: He's moving into beer.

BUTCHER: Okay?

DOGSBOROUGH: I certainly appreciate

Your oldtime sentiments, but no one gives
Away a shipyard for a song.

FLAKE: There's something
In that. But now the loan has fallen through
Maybe the twenty thousand will come in handy.

BUTCHER: And possibly right now we're not too eager
To throw our stock upon the open market . . .

DOGSBOROUGH: That sounds more like it. Not a bad deal if
It's got no strings attached.

FLAKE: None whatsoever.

DOGSBOROUGH: The price you say is twenty thousand?

FLAKE: Is it
Too much?

DOGSBOROUGH: No. And imagine, it's the selfsame
Shipyard where years ago I opened my first lunchroom.
As long as there's no nigger in the woodpile . . .
You've really given up the loan?

FLAKE: Completely.

DOGSBOROUGH: I might consider it. Hey, look here, son
It's just the thing for you. I thought you fellows
Were down on me and here you make this offer.
You see, my boy, that honesty sometimes
Pays off. It's like you say: When I pass on
The youngster won't inherit much more than
My name, and these old eyes have seen what evil
Can spring from penury.

BUTCHER: We'll feel much better
If you accept. The ugly aftertaste
Left by our foolish proposition would be
Dispelled. In future we could benefit
By your advice. You'd show us how to ride
The slump by honest means, because our business
Would be your business, Dogsborough, because
You too would be a cauliflower man
And want the Cauliflower Trust to win.

Dogsborough takes his hand.

DOGSBOROUGH: Butcher and Flake, I'm in.
YOUNG DOGSBOROUGH: My father's in.
  A sign appears.

3

*Bookmaker's office on 122nd Street. Arturo Ui and his lieutenant
Ernesto Roma, accompanied by bodyguards, are listening to the
racing news on the radio. Next to Roma is Dockdaisy.*

ROMA: I wish, Arturo, you could cure yourself
  Of this black melancholy, this inactive
  Dreaming. The whole town's talking.
UI, *bitterly*:   Talking? Who's talking?
  Nobody talks about me any more.
  This city's got no memory. Short-lived
  Is fame in such a place. Two months without
  A murder, and a man's forgotten.
  He whisks through the newspapers.
                           When
  The rod falls silent, silence strikes the press.
  Even when I deliver murders by the
  Dozen, I'm never sure they'll print them.
  It's not accomplishment that counts; it's
  Influence, which in turn depends on my
  Bank balance. Things have come to such a pass
  I sometimes think of chucking the whole business.
ROMA: The boys are chafing too from lack of cash.
  Morale is low. This inactivity's
  No good for them. A man with nothing but
  The ace of spades to shoot at goes to seed.
  I feel so sorry for those boys, Arturo
  I hate to show my face at headquarters. When
  They look at me, my 'Tomorrow we'll see action'

Sticks in my throat. Your vegetables idea was
So promising. Why don't we start right in?
UI: Not now. Not from the bottom. It's too soon.
ROMA: 'Too soon' is good. For four months now—
Remember? – since the Cauliflower Trust
Gave you the brush-off, you've been idly brooding.
Plans! Plans! Half-hearted feelers! That rebuff
Frizzled your spine. And then that little mishap –
Those cops at Harper's Bank – you've never gotten
Over it.
UI: But they fired!
ROMA: Only in
The air. That was illegal.
UI: Still too close
For me. I'd be in stir if they had plugged
My only witness. And that judge! Not two
Cent's worth of sympathy.
ROMA: The cops won't shoot
For grocery stores. They shoot for banks. Look here
Arturo, we'll start on Eleventh Street
Smash a few windows, wreck the furniture
Pour kerosene on the veg. And then we work
Our way to Seventh. Two or three days later
Giri, a posy in his buttonhole
Drops in and offers our protection for
A suitable percentage on their sales.
UI: No. First I need protection for myself
From cops and judges. Then I'll start to think
About protecting other people. We've
Got to start from the top.
Gloomily:
                          Until I've put the
Judge in my pocket by slipping something
Of mine in his, the law's against me. I
Can't even rob a bank without some two-bit cop
Shooting me dead.

ROMA: You're right. Our only hope is
   Givola's plan. He's got a nose for smells
   And if he says the Cauliflower Trust
   Smells promisingly rotten, I believe
   There's something in it. And there *was* some talk
   When, as they say, on Dogsborough's commendation
   The city made that loan. Since then I've heard
   Rumours about some docks that aren't being built
   But ought to be. Yet on the other hand
   Dogsborough recommended it. Why should
   That do-good peg for fishy business? Here comes
   Ragg of the 'Star'. If anybody knows
   About such things, it's him. Hi Ted.
RAGG, *slightly drunk*:   Hi, boys!
   Hi, Roma! Hi, Arturo! How are things in
   Capua?
UI: What's he saying?
RAGG: Oh, nothing much.
   That was a one-horse town where long ago
   An army went to pot from idleness
   And easy living.
UI: Go to hell!
ROMA, *to Ragg*:   No fighting.
   Tell us about that loan the Cauliflower
   Trust wangled.
RAGG: What do you care? Say! Could you
   Be going into vegetables? I've got it!
   You're angling for a loan yourselves. See Dogsborough.
   He'll put it through.
   Imitating the old man:
                    'Can we allow a business
   Basically sound but momentarily
   Threatened with blight, to perish?' Not an eye
   At City Hall but fills with tears. Deep feeling
   For cauliflower shakes the council members
   As though it were a portion of themselves.

Too bad, Arturo, guns call forth no tears.
The other customers laugh.

ROMA: Don't bug him, Ted. He's out of sorts.

RAGG: I shouldn't
Wonder. I hear that Givola has been
To see Capone for a job.

DOCKDAISY: You liar!
You leave Giuseppe out of this!

RAGG: Hi, Dockdaisy!
Still got your place in Shorty Givola's harem?
Introducing her:
Fourth super in the harem of the third
Lieutenant of a –
Points to Ui.
                    – fast declining star
Of second magnitude! Oh, bitter fate!

DOCKDAISY: Somebody shut the rotten bastard up!

RAGG: Posterity plaits no laurels for the gangster!
New heroes captivate the fickle crowd.
Yesterday's hero has been long forgotten
His mug-shot gathers dust in ancient files.
'Don't you remember, folks, the wounds I gave you?' –
'When?' – 'Once upon a time.' – 'Those wounds have
Turned to scars long since.' Alas, the finest scars
Get lost with those who bear them. 'Can it be
That in a world where good deeds go unnoticed
No monument remains to evil ones?' –
'Yes, so it is.' – 'Oh, lousy world!'

UI, *bellows*:   Shut
Him up!
The bodyguards approach Ragg.

RAGG, *turning pale*: Be careful, Ui. Don't insult
The press.
The other customers have risen to their feet in alarm.

ROMA: You'd better beat it, Ted. You've said
Too much already.

RAGG, *backing out, now very much afraid*:
>   See you later, boys.
The room empties quickly.

ROMA: Your nerves are shot, Arturo.

UI: Those bastards
  Treat me like dirt.

ROMA: Because of your long silence.
  No other reason.

UI, *gloomily*:   Say, what's keeping Giri
  And that accountant from the Cauliflower
  Trust?

ROMA: They were due at three.

UI: And Givola?
  What's this I hear about him seeing Capone?

ROMA: Nothing at all. He's in his flower shop
  Minding his business, and Capone comes in
  To buy some wreaths.

UI: Some wreaths? For who?

ROMA: Not us.

UI: I'm not so sure.

ROMA: You're seeing things too black.
  Nobody's interested in us.

UI: Exactly.
  They've more respect for dirt. Take Givola.
  One setback and he blows. By God
  I'll settle his account when things look up.

ROMA: Giri!
Enter Emanuele Giri with a rundown individual, Bowl.

GIRI: I've got him, boss.

ROMA, *to Bowl*:   They tell me you
  Are Sheet's accountant at the Cauliflower
  Trust.

BOWL: Was. Until last week that bastard . . .

GIRI: He hates the very smell of cauliflower.

BOWL: Dogsborough . . .

UI, *quickly*:   Dogsborough! What about him?

ROMA: What have you got to do with Dogsborough?
GIRI: That's why I brought him.
BOWL: Dogsborough
Fired me.
ROMA: He fired you? From Sheet's shipyard?
BOWL: No, from his own. He took it over on
September first.
ROMA: What's that?
GIRI: Sheet's shipyard
Belongs to Dogsborough. Bowl here was present
When Butcher of the Cauliflower Trust
Handed him fifty-one percent of the stock.
UI: So what?
BOWL: So what? It's scandalous . . .
GIRI   Don't you
Get it, boss?
BOWL: . . . Dogsborough sponsoring that
Loan to the Cauliflower Trust . . .
GIRI: . . . when he
Himself was secretly a member of
The Cauliflower Trust.
UI, *who is beginning to see the light*:
                              Say, that's corrupt.
By God the old man hasn't kept his nose
Too clean.
BOWL: The loan was to the Cauliflower
Trust, but they did it through the shipyard. Through
Me. And I signed for Dogsborough. Not for Sheet
As people thought.
GIRI: By golly, it's a killer.
Old Dogsborough. The trusty and reliable
Signboard. So honest. So responsible!
Whose handshake was an honour and a pledge!
The staunch and incorruptible old man!
BOWL: I'll make the bastard pay. Can you imagine?
Firing me for embezzlement when he himself . . .

ROMA: Cool it! You're not the only one whose blood
  Boils at such abject villainy. What do
  You say, Arturo?
UI, *referring to Bowl*:
                    Will he testify?
GIRI: He'll testify.
UI, *grandly getting ready to leave*:
                          Keep an eye on him, boys. Let's go
  Roma. I smell an opening.
  *He goes out quickly, followed by Ernesto Roma and the body-
  guards.*
GIRI, *slaps Bowl on the back*: Bowl, I
  Believe you've set a wheel in motion, which . . .
BOWL: I hope you'll pay me back for any loss . . .
GIRI: Don't worry about that. I know the boss.
  A sign appears.

4

Dogsborough's country house. Dogsborough and his son.

DOGSBOROUGH: I should never have accepted this estate.
  Taking that package as a kind of gift was
  Beyond reproach.
YOUNG DOGSBOROUGH: Of course it was.
DOGSBOROUGH: And sponsoring
  That loan, when I discovered to my own
  Detriment that a thriving line of business
  Was languishing for lack of funds, was hardly
  Dishonest. But when, confident the shipyard
  Would yield a handsome profit, I accepted
  This house before I moved the loan, so secretly
  Acting in my own interest – that was wrong.
YOUNG DOGSBOROUGH: Yes, father.

DOGSBOROUGH: That was faulty judgment
   Or might be so regarded. Yes, my boy
   I should never have accepted this estate.

YOUNG DOGSBOROUGH: No.

DOGSBOROUGH: We've stepped into a trap.

YOUNG DOGSBOROUGH: Yes, father.

DOGSBOROUGH: That
   Package of stocks was like the salty titbit
   They serve free gratis at the bar to make
   The customer, appeasing his cheap hunger
   Work up a raging thirst.
   Pause.

                    That inquiry
   At City Hall about the docks, has got
   Me down. The loan's used up. Clark helped
   Himself; so did Caruther, Flake and Butcher
   And so, I'm sad to say, did I. And no
   Cement's been bought yet, not a pound! The one
   Good thing is this: at Sheet's request I kept
   The deal a secret; no one knows of my
   Connection with the shipyard.

A BUTLER *enters*:   Telephone
   Sir, Mr Butcher of the Cauliflower
   Trust.

DOGSBOROUGH: Take it, son.
   Young Dogsborough goes out with the Butler. Church bells are
   heard in the distance.

DOGSBOROUGH   Now what can Butcher want?
   Looking out of the window.
   Those poplars are what tempted me to take
   The place. The poplars and the lake down there, like
   Silver before it's minted into dollars.
   And air that's free of beer fumes. The fir trees
   Are good to look at too, especially
   The tops. Grey-green and dusty. And the trunks –

Their colour calls to mind the leathers we used to wrap
   around
The taps when drawing beer. It was the poplars, though
That turned the trick. Ah yes, the poplars.
It's Sunday. Hm. The bells would sound so peaceful
If the world were not so full of wickedness.
But what can Butcher want on Sunday?
I never should have . . .

YOUNG DOGSBOROUGH, *returning*: Father, Butcher says
Last night the City Council voted to
Investigate the Cauliflower Trust's
Projected docks. Father, what's wrong?

DOGSBOROUGH: My smelling salts!

YOUNG DOGSBOROUGH, *gives them to him*:
Here.

DOGSBOROUGH: What does Butcher want?

YOUNG DOGSBOROUGH: He wants to come here.

DOGSBOROUGH: Here? I refuse to see him. I'm not well.
My heart.
He stands up. Grandly:
I haven't anything to do
With this affair. For sixty years I've trodden
The narrow path, as everybody knows.
They can't involve me in their schemes.

YOUNG DOGSBOROUGH: No, father.
Do you feel better now?

THE BUTLER *enters*:   A Mr Ui
Desires to see you, sir.

DOGSBOROUGH: The gangster!

THE BUTLER: Yes
I've seen his picture in the papers. Says he
Was sent by Mr Clark of the Cauliflower
Trust.

DOGSBOROUGH:
Throw him out! Who sent him? Clark? Good God!
Is he threatening me with gangsters now? I'll . . . .

Enter Arturo Ui and Ernesto Roma.

UI: Mr
Dogsborough.

DOGSBOROUGH: Get out!

ROMA: I wouldn't be in such
A hurry, friend. It's Sunday. Take it easy.

DOGSBOROUGH: Get out, I said!

YOUNG DOGSBOROUGH: My father says: Get out!

ROMA: Saying it twice won't make it any smarter.

UI, *unruffled*:
Mr Dogsborough.

DOGSBOROUGH: Where are the servants? Call the
Police.

ROMA: I wouldn't leave the room if I
Were you, son. In the hallway you might run
Into some boys who wouldn't understand.

DOGSBOROUGH: Ho! Violence!

ROMA: I wouldn't call it that.
Only a little emphasis perhaps.

UI: Mr Dogsborough. I am well aware that you
Don't know me, or even worse, you know me but
Only from hearsay. Mr Dogsborough
I have been very much maligned, my image
Blackened by envy, my intentions disfigured
By baseness. When some fourteen years ago
Yours truly, then a modest, unemployed
Son of the Bronx, appeared within the gates
Of this your city to launch a new career
Which, I may say, has not been utterly
Inglorious, my only followers
Were seven youngsters, penniless like myself
But brave and like myself determined
To cut their chunk of meat from every cow
The Lord created. I've got thirty now
And will have more. But now you're wondering: What
Does Arturo Ui want of me? Not much. Just this.

What irks me is to be misunderstood
To be regarded as a fly-by-night
Adventurer and heaven knows what else.
Clears his throat.
Especially by the police, for I
Esteem them and I'd welcome their esteem.
And so I've come to ask you – and believe me
Asking's not easy for my kind of man –
To put a word in for me with the precinct
When necessary.

DOGSBOROUGH, *incredulously*:
                              Vouch for you, you mean?
UI: If necessary. That depends on whether
  We strike a friendly understanding with
  The vegetable dealers.
DOGSBOROUGH: What is your
  Connection with the vegetable trade?
UI: That's what I'm coming to. The vegetable
  Trade needs protection. By force if necessary.
  And I'm determined to supply it.
DOGSBOROUGH: No
  One's theatening it as far as I can see.
UI: Maybe not. Not yet. But I see further. And
  I ask you: How long with our corrupt police
  Force will the vegetable dealer be allowed
  To sell his vegetables in peace? A ruthless
  Hand may destroy his little shop tomorrow
  And make off with his cash-box. Would he not
  Prefer at little cost to arm himself
  Before the trouble starts, with powerful protection?
DOGSBOROUGH: I doubt it.
UI: That would mean he doesn't know
  What's good for him. Quite possible. The small
  Vegetable dealer, honest but short-sighted
  Hard-working but too often unaware
  Of his best interest, needs strong leadership.

Moreover, toward the Cauliflower Trust
That gave him everything he has, he feels
No sense of responsibility. That's where I
Come in again. The Cauliflower Trust
Must likewise be protected. Down with the welshers!
Pay up, say I, or close your shop! The weak
Will perish. Let them, that's the law of nature.
In short, the Trust requires my services.

DOGSBOROUGH: But what's the Cauliflower Trust to me?
Why come to me with this amazing plan?

UI: We'll get to that. I'll tell you what you need.
The Cauliflower Trust needs muscle, thirty
Determined men under my leadership.

DOGSBOROUGH:
Whether the Trust would want to change its typewriters
For tommy-guns I have no way of knowing.
You see, I'm not connected with the Trust.

UI: We'll get to that. You say: With thirty men
Armed to the teeth, at home on our premises
How do we know that we ourselves are safe?
The answer's very simple. He who holds
The purse strings holds the power. And it's you
Who hand out the pay envelopes. How could
I turn against you even if I wanted
Even without the high esteem I bear you?
For what do I amount to? What
Following have I got? A handful. And some
Are dropping out. Right now it's twenty. Or less.
Without your help I'm finished. It's your duty
Your human duty to protect me from
My enemies, and (I may as well be frank)
My followers too! The work of fourteen years
Hangs in the balance! I appeal to you
As man to man.

DOGSBOROUGH: As man to man I'll tell
You what I'll do. I'm calling the police.

UI: What? The police?

DOGSBOROUGH: Exactly, the police!

UI: Am I to understand that you refuse
   To help me as a man?
   Bellows.

                    Then I demand
   It of you as a criminal. Because
   That's what you are. I'm going to expose you.
   I've got the proofs. There's going to be a scandal
   About some docks. And you're mixed up in it. Sheet's
   Shipyard – that's you. I'm warning you! Don't
   Push me too far! They've voted to investigate.

DOGSBOROUGH, *very pale*:
   They never will. They can't. My friends . . .

UI: You haven't got any. You had some yesterday.
   Today you haven't got a single friend
   Tomorrow you'll have nothing but enemies.
   If anybody can rescue you, it's me
   Arturo Ui! Me! Me!

DOGSBOROUGH: Nobody's going to
   Investigate. My hair is white.

UI: But nothing else
   Is white about you, Dogsborough.
   Tries to seize his hand.
   Think, man! It's now or never. Let me save you!
   One word from you and any bastard who
   Touches a hair of yon white head, I'll drill him.
   Dogsborough, help me now. I beg you. Once.
   Just once! Oh, say the word, or I shall never
   Be able to face my boys again.
   He weeps.

DOGSBOROUGH: Never!
   I'd sooner die than get mixed up with you.

UI: I'm washed up and I know it. Forty
   And still a nobody. You've got to help me.

DOGSBOROUGH: Never.

UI: I'm warning you. I'll crush you.

DOGSBOROUGH: Never
Never while I draw breath will you get away with
Your green goods racket.

UI, *with dignity*: Mr Dogsborough
I'm only forty. You are eighty. With God's
Help I'll outlast you. And one thing I know:
I'll break into the green goods business yet.

DOGSBOROUGH: Never!

UI: Come, Roma. Let's get out of here.

He makes a formal bow and leaves the room with Ernesto Roma.

DOGSBOROUGH: Air! Give me air. Oh, what a mug!
Oh, what a mug! I should never have accepted
This estate. But they won't dare. I'm sunk
If they investigate, but they won't dare.

THE BUTLER *enters*: Goodwill and Gaffles of the city
council.

Enter Goodwill and Gaffles.

GOODWILL: Hello, Dogsborough.

DOGSBOROUGH: Hello, Goodwill and Gaffles.
Anything new?

GOODWILL: Plenty, and not so good, I fear.
But wasn't that Arturo Ui who
Just passed us in the hall?

DOGSBOROUGH, *with a forced laugh*: Himself in person.
Hardly an ornament to a country home.

GOODWILL: No.
Hardly an ornament. It's no good wind
That brings us. It's that loan we made the Trust
To build their docks with.

DOGSBOROUGH, *stiffly*: What about the loan?

GAFFLES: Well, certain council members said – don't get
Upset – the thing looked kind of fishy.

DOGSBOROUGH: Fishy.

GOODWILL: Don't worry The majority flew off
The handle. Fishy! We almost came to blows.

GAFFLES: Dogsborough's contracts fishy! they shouted.
   What
   About the Bible? Is that fishy too?
   It almost turned to an ovation for you
   Dogsborough. When your friends demanded an
   Investigation, some, infected with
   Our confidence, withdrew their motion and
   Wanted to shelve the whole affair. But the
   Majority, resolved to clear your name
   Of every vestige of suspicion, shouted:
   Dogsborough's more than a name. It stands for more
       than
   A man. It's an institution! In an uproar
   They voted the investigation.

DOGSBOROUGH: The
   Investigation.

GOODWILL: O'Casey is in charge.
   The cauliflower people merely say
   The loan was made directly to Sheet's shipyard.
   The contracts with the builders were to be
   Negotiated by Sheet's shipyard.

DOGSBOROUGH: By Sheet's shipyard.

GOODWILL: The best would be for you to send a man
   Of flawless reputation and impartiality
   Someone you trust, to throw some light on this
   Unholy rat's nest.

DOGSBOROUGH: So I will.

GAFFLES: All right
   That settles it. And now suppose you show us
   This famous country house of yours. We'll want
   To tell our friends about it.

DOGSBOROUGH: Very well.

GOODWILL:
   What blessed peace! And church bells! All one can
   Wish for.

GAFFLES, *laughing*:
>   No docks in sight.

DOGSBOROUGH: I'll send a man.
  They go out slowly.
  A sign appears.

5

City Hall. Butcher, Flake, Clark, Mulberry, Caruther. Across from them Dogsborough, who is as white as a sheet, O'Casey, Gaffles and Goodwill. Reporters.

BUTCHER, *in an undertone*:
  He's late.

MULBERRY: He's bringing Sheet. Quite possibly
  They haven't come to an agreement. I
  Believe they've been discussing it all night.
  Sheet *has* to say the shipyard still belongs
  To him.

CARUTHER: It's asking quite a lot of Sheet
  To come here just to tell us *he's* the scoundrel.

FLAKE: He'll never come.

CLARK: He's got to.

FLAKE: Why should he
  Ask to be sent to prison for five years?

CLARK: It's quite a pile of dough. And Mabel Sheet
  Needs luxury. He's still head over heels
  In love with Mabel. He'll play ball all right.
  And anyway he'll never serve his term.
  Old Dogsborough will see to that.
  The shouts of newsboys are heard. A reporter brings in a paper.

GAFFLES: Sheet's been found dead. In his hotel. A ticket
  To San Francisco in his pocket.

BUTCHER: Sheet
  Dead?

O'CASEY, *reading*:
        Murdered.

MULBERRY: My God!

FLAKE, *in an undertone*:   He didn't come.

GAFFLES: What is it, Dogsborough?

DOGSBOROUGH, *speaking with difficulty*:

                          Nothing. It'll pass.

O'CASEY: Sheet's death . . .

CLARK: Poor Sheet. His unexpected death
  Would seem to puncture your investigation . . .

O'CASEY: Of course the unexpected often looks
  As if it were expected. Some indeed
  Expect the unexpected. Such is life.
  This leaves me in a pretty pickle and
  I hope you won't refer me and my questions
  To Sheet; for Sheet, according to this paper
  Has been most silent since last night.

MULBERRY: Your questions?
  You know the loan was given to the shipyard
  Don't you?

O'CASEY: Correct. But there remains a question:
  Who is the shipyard?

FLAKE, *under his breath*: Funny question! He's
  Got something up his sleeve.

CLARK, *likewise*:   I wonder what.

O'CASEY:
  Something wrong, Dogsborough? Could it be the air?
  To the others.
  I only mean: some people may be thinking
  That several shovelsful of earth are not
  Enough to load on Sheet, and certain muck
  Might just as well be added. I suspect . . .

CLARK: Maybe you'd better not suspect too much

O'Casey. Ever hear of slander? We've
Got laws agaist it.

MULBERRY: What's the point of these
Insinuations? Dogsborough, they tell me
Has picked a man to clear this business up.
Let's wait until he comes.

O'CASEY: He's late. And when
He comes, I hope Sheet's not the only thing
He'll talk about.

FLAKE: We hope he'll tell the truth
No more no less.

O'CASEY: You mean the man is honest?
That suits me fine. Since Sheet was still alive
Last night, the whole thing should be clear. I only –
To Dogsborough.
– Hope that you've chosen a good man.

CLARK, *cuttingly*:   You'll have
To take him as he is. Ah, here he comes.
Enter Arturo Ui and Ernesto Roma with bodyguards.

UI: Hi, Clark! Hi, Dogsborough! Hi, everybody!

CLARK: Hi, Ui.

UI: Well, it seems you've got some questions.

O'CASEY, *to Dogsborough*:
Is this your man?

CLARK: That's right, Not good enough?

GOODWILL: Dogsborough, can you be . . . ?
Commotion among the reporters.

O'CASEY: Quiet over there!

A REPORTER: It's Ui!
*Laughter. O'Casey bangs his gavel for order. Then he musters
the bodyguards.*

O'CASEY: Who are these men?

UI: Friends.

O'CASEY, *to Roma*:   And who
Are you?

UI: Ernesto Roma, my accountant.

GAFFLES: Hold it! Can you be serious, Dogsborough?
Dogsborough is silent.
O'CASEY: Mr
Ui, we gather from Mr Dogsborough's
Eloquent silence that you have his confidence
And desire ours. Well then. Where are the contracts?
UI: What contracts?
CLARK, *seeing that O'Casey is looking at Goodwill*:
                    The contracts that the shipyard no doubt
Signed with the builders with a view to enlarging
Its dock facilities.
UI: I never heard
Of any contracts.
O'CASEY: Really?
CLARK: Do you mean
There are no contracts?
O'CASEY, *quickly*:   Did you talk with Sheet?
UI, *shaking his head*:
No.
CLARK: Oh. You didn't talk with Sheet?
UI, *angrily*:   If any-
One says I talked with Sheet, that man's a liar.
O'CASEY: Ui, I thought that Mr Dogsborough
Had asked you to look into this affair?
UI: I have looked into it.
O'CASEY: And have your studies
Borne fruit?
UI: They have. It wasn't easy to
Lay bare the truth. And it's not a pleasant truth.
When Mr Dogsborough, in the interest of
This city, asked me to investigate
Where certain city funds, the hard-earned savings
Of taxpayers like you and me, entrusted
To a certain shipyard in this city, had gone to
I soon discovered to my consternation
That they had been embezzled. That's Point One.

Point Two is who embezzled them. All right
I'll answer that one too. The guilty party
Much as it pains me is . . .

O'CASEY: Well, who is it?

UI: Sheet.

O'CASEY: Oh, Sheet! The silent Sheet you didn't talk to!

UI: Why look at me like that? The guilty party
Is Sheet.

CLARK: Sheet's dead. Didn't you know?

UI: What, dead?
I was in Cicero last night. That's why
I haven't heard. And Roma here was with me.
Pause.

ROMA: That's mighty funny. Do you think it's mere
Coincidence that . . .

UI: Gentlemen, it's not
An accident. Sheet's suicide was plainly
The consequence of Sheet's embezzlement.
It's monstrous!

O'CASEY: Except it wasn't suicide.

UI: What then? Of course Ernesto here and I
Were in Cicero last night. We wouldn't know.
But this we know beyond a doubt: that Sheet
Apparently an honest businessman
Was just a gangster.

O'CASEY: Ui, I get your drift.
You can't find words too damaging for Sheet
After the damage he incurred last night.
Well, Dogsborough, let's get to you.

DOGSBOROUGH: To me?

BUTCHER, *cuttingly*:
What about Dogsborough?

O'CASEY: As I understand Mr
Ui – and I believe I understand
Him very well – there was a shipyard which
Borrowed some money which has disappeared.

But now the question rises: Who is this
Shipyard? It's Sheet, you say. But what's a name?
What interests us right now is not its name
But whom it actually belonged to. Did it
Belong to Sheet? Unquestionably Sheet
Could tell us. But Sheet has buttoned up
About his property since Ui spent
The night in Cicero. But could it be
That when this swindle was put over someone
Else was the owner? What is your opinion
Dogsborough?

DOGSBOROUGH: Me?

O'CASEY: Yes, could it be that you
Were sitting in Sheet's office when a contract
Was ... well, suppose we say, not being drawn up?

GOODWILL: O'Casey!

GAFFLES, *to O'Casey*:
                    Dogsborough? You're crazy!

DOGSBOROUGH: I ...

O'CASEY: And earlier, at City Hall, when you
Told us how hard a time the cauliflower
People were having and how badly they
Needed a loan – could that have been the voice
Of personal involvement?

BUTCHER: Have you no shame?
The man's unwell.

CARUTHER: Consider his great age!

FLAKE:
His snow-white hair confounds your low suspicions.

ROMA: Where are your proofs?

O'CASEY: The proofs are ...

UI   Quiet, please!
Let's have a little quiet, friends.
Say something, Dogsborough!

A BODYGUARD, *suddenly roars*: The chief wants quiet!
Quiet!

Sudden silence.

UI: If I may say what moves me in
This hour and at this shameful sight – a white-
Haired man insulted while his friends look on
In silence – it is this. I trust you, Mr
Dogsborough. And I ask: Is this the face
Of guilt? Is this the eye of one who follows
Devious ways? Can you no longer
Distinguish white from black? A pretty pass
If things have come to such a pass!

CLARK: A man of
Untarnished reputation is accused
Of bribery.

O'CASEY: And more: of fraud. For I
Contend that this unholy shipyard, so
Maligned when Sheet was thought to be the owner
Belonged to Dogsborough at the time the loan
Went through.

MULBERRY: A filthy lie!

CARUTHER: I'll stake my head
For Dogsborough. Summon the population!
I challenge you to find one man to doubt him.

A REPORTER, *to another who has come in*:
Dogsborough's under suspicion.

THE OTHER REPORTER: Dogsborough?
Why not Abe Lincoln?

MULBERRY *and* FLAKE: Witnesses!

O'CASEY: Oh
It's witnesses you want? Hey, Smith, where *is*
Our witness? Is he here? I see he is.
One of his men has stepped into the doorway and made a sign.
All look toward the door. Short pause. Then a burst of shots
and noise are heard. Tumult. The reporters run out.

THE REPORTERS: It's outside. A machine-gun. – What's
your witness's name, O'Casey? – Bad business. – Hi, Ui!

O'CASEY, *going to the door*: Bowl! *Shouts out the door*. Come
  on in!

THE MEN OF THE CAULIFLOWER TRUST: What's going
  on? – Somebody's been shot – On the stairs – God damn it!

BUTCHER, *to Ui*:
  More monkey business? Ui, it's all over
  Between us if . . .

UI: Yes?

O'CASEY: Bring him in!
  Policemen carry in a corpse.

O'CASEY: It's Bowl. My witness, gentlemen, I fear
  Is not in a fit state for questioning.
  *He goes out quickly. The policemen have set down Bowl's body
  in a corner.*

DOGSBOROUGH:
  For God's sake, Gaffles, get me out of here!
  Without answering Gaffles goes out past him.

UI, *going toward Dogsborough with outstretched hand*:
  Congratulations, Dogsborough. Don't doubt
  One way or another, I'll get things straightened out.
  A sign appears.

6

*Hotel Mammoth. Ui's suite. Two bodyguards lead a ragged actor
  to Ui. In the background Givola.*

FIRST BODYGUARD: It's an actor, boss. Unarmed.

SECOND BODYGUARD: He can't afford a rod. He was able to
  get tight because they pay him to declaim in the saloons
  when they're tight. But I'm told that he's good. He's one
  of them classical guys.

UI: Okay. Here's the problem. I've been given to understand
  that my pronunciation leaves something to be desired. It

looks like I'm going to have to say a word or two on
certain occasions, especially when I get into politics, so
I've decided to take lessons. The gestures too.

THE ACTOR: Very well.

UI: Get the mirror.

A bodyguard comes front stage with a large standing mirror.

UI: First the walk. How do you guys walk in the theatre or
the opera?

THE ACTOR: I see what you mean. The grand style. Julius
Caesar, Hamlet, Romeo – that's Shakespeare. Mr Ui,
you've come to the right man. Old Mahonney can teach
you the classical manner in ten minutes. Gentlemen, you
see before you a tragic figure. Ruined by Shakespeare. An
English poet. If it weren't for Shakespeare, I could be on
Broadway right now. The tragedy of a character. 'Don't
play Shakespeare when you're playing Ibsen, Mahonney!
Look at the calendar! This is 1912, sir!' – 'Art knows no
calendar, sir!' say I. 'And art is my life.' Alas.

GIVOLA: I think you've got the wrong guy, boss. He's out
of date.

UI: We'll see about that. Walk around like they do in this
Shakespeare.

The actor walks around.

UI: Good!

GIVOLA: You can't walk like that in front of cauliflower
men. It ain't natural.

UI: What do you mean it ain't natural? Nobody's natural in
this day and age. When I walk I want people to know
I'm walking.

He copies the actor's gait.

THE ACTOR: Head back. *Ui throws his head back.* The foot
touches the ground toe first. *Ui's foot touches the ground toe
first.* Good. Excellent. You have a natural gift. Only the
arms. They're not quite right. Stiff. Perhaps if you joined
your arms in front of your private parts. *Ui joins his arms in
front of his private parts.* Not bad. Relaxed but firm. But

head back. Good. Just the right gait for your purposes, I
believe, Mr Ui. What else do you wish to learn?

UI: How to stand. In front of people.

GIVOLA: Have two big bruisers right behind you and you'll
be standing pretty.

UI: That's bunk. When I stand I don't want people looking
at the two bozos behind me. I want them looking at me.
Correct me!

He takes a stance, his arms crossed over his chest.

THE ACTOR: A possible solution. But common. You don't
want to look like a barber, Mr Ui. Fold your arms like this.
*He folds his arms in such a way that the backs of his hands
remain visible. His palms are resting on his arms not far from
the shoulder.* A trifling change, but the difference is in-
calculable. Draw the comparison in the mirror, Mr Ui.
Ui tries out the new position before the mirror.

UI: Not bad.

GIVOLA: What's all this for, boss? Just for those
Fancy-pants in the Trust?

UI: Hell, no! It's for
The little people. Why, for instance, do
You think this Clark makes such a show of grandeur?
Not for his peers. His bank account
Takes care of them, the same as my big bruisers
Lend me prestige in certain situations.
Clark makes a show of grandeur to impress
The little man. I mean to do the same.

GIVOLA: But some will say it doesn't look inborn.
Some people stick at that.

UI: I know they do.
But I'm not trying to convince professors
And smart-alecks. My object is the little
Man's image of his master.

GIVOLA: Don't overdo
The master, boss. Better the democrat
The friendly, reassuring type in shirtsleeves.

UI: I've got old Dogsborough for that.

GIVOLA: His image
Is kind of tarnished, I should say. He's still
An asset on the books, a venerable
Antique. But people aren't as eager as they
Were to exhibit him. They're not so sure
He's genuine. It's like the family Bible
Nobody opens any more since, piously
Turning the yellowed pages with a group
Of friends, they found a dried-out bedbug. But
Maybe he's good enough for Cauliflower.

UI: I decide who's respectable.

GIVOLA: Sure thing, boss.
There's nothing wrong with Dogsborough. We can
Still use him. They haven't even dropped him
At City Hall. The crash would be too loud.

UI: Sitting.

THE ACTOR: Sitting. Sitting is almost the hardest, Mr Ui.
There are men who can walk; there are men who can
stand; but find me a man who can sit. Take a chair with a
back-rest, Mr Ui. But don't lean against it. Hands on thighs,
level with the abdomen, elbows away from body. How
long can you sit like that, Mr Ui?

UI: As long as I please.

THE ACTOR: Then everything's perfect, Mr Ui.

GIVOLA: You know, boss, when old Dogsborough passes
    on
Giri could take his place. He's got the
Popular touch. He plays the funny man
And laughs so loud in season that the plaster
Comes tumbling from the ceiling. Sometimes, though
He does it out of season, as for instance
When you step forward as the modest son of
The Bronx you really were and talk about
Those seven determined youngsters.

UI: Then he laughs?

GIVOLA: The plaster tumbles from the ceiling. Don't
　　Tell him I said so or he'll think I've got
　　It in for him. But maybe you could make
　　Him stop collecting hats.
UI:　　　　　　　　　　　　What kind of hats?
GIVOLA: The hats of people he's rubbed out. And running
　　Around with them in public. It's disgusting.
UI: Forget it. I would never think of muzzling
　　The ox that treads my corn. I overlook
　　The petty foibles of my underlings.
　　To the actor.
　　And now to speaking! Speak a speech for me!
THE ACTOR: Shakespeare. Nothing else. Julius Caesar. The
　　Roman hero. *He draws a little book from his pocket.* What
　　do you say to Mark Antony's speech? Over Caesar's body.
　　Against Brutus. The ringleader of Caesar's assassins. A
　　model of demagogy. Very famous. I played Antony in
　　Zenith in 1908. Just what you need, Mr Ui. *He takes a
　　stance and recites Mark Antony's speech line for line.*
　　Friends, Romans, countrymen, lend me your ears!
　　*Reading from the little book, Ui speaks the lines after him. Now
　　and then the actor corrects him, but in the main Ui keeps his
　　rough staccato delivery.*
THE ACTOR: I come to bury Caesar, not to praise him.
　　The evil that men do lives after them;
　　The good is oft interred with their bones;
　　So let it be with Caesar. The noble Brutus
　　Hath told you Caesar was ambitious.
　　If it were so, it was a grievous fault,
　　And grievously hath Caesar answer'd it.
UI, *continues by himself*:
　　Here, under leave of Brutus and the rest –
　　For Brutus is an honourable man;
　　So are they all, all honourable men –
　　Come I to speak in Caesar's funeral.
　　He was my friend, faithful and just to me;

But Brutus says he was ambitious;
And Brutus is an honourable man.
He hath brought many captives home to Rome,
Whose ransoms did the general coffers fill;
Did this in Caesar seem ambitious?
When that the poor have cried, Caesar hath wept;
Ambition should be made of sterner stuff.
Yet Brutus says he was ambitious;
And Brutus is an honourable man.
You all did see that on the Lupercal
I thrice presented him a kingly crown,
Which he did thrice refuse. Was this ambition?
Yet Brutus says he was ambitious;
And sure he is an honourable man.
I speak not to disprove what Brutus spoke,
But here I am to speak what I do know.
You all did love him once, not without cause?
What cause withholds you then, to mourn for him?
During the last lines the curtain slowly falls.
A sign appears.

7

Offices of the Cauliflower Trust. Arturo Ui, Ernesto Roma, Giuseppe Givola, Emanuele Giri and bodyguards. A group of small vegetable dealers is listening to Ui. Old Dogsborough, who is ill, is sitting on the platform beside Ui. In the background Clark.

UI, *bellowing*: Murder! Extortion! Highway robbery!
  Machine-guns sputtering on our city streets!
  People going about their business, law-abiding
  Citizens on their way to City Hall
  To make a statement, murdered in broad daylight!
  And what, I ask you, do our town fathers do?

Nothing! These honourable men are much
Too busy planning their shady little deals
And slandering respectable citizens
To think of law enforcement.

GIVOLA: Hear!

UI: In short
Chaos is rampant. Because if everybody
Can do exactly what he pleases, if
Dog can eat dog without a second thought
I call it chaos. Look. Suppose I'm sitting
Peacefully in my vegetable store
For instance, or driving my cauliflower truck
And someone comes barging not so peacefully
Into my store: 'Hands up!' Or with his gun
Punctures my tyres. Under such conditions
Peace is unthinkable. But once I know
The score, once I recognise that men are not
Innocent lambs, then I've got to find a way
To stop these men from smashing up my shop and
Making me, when it suits them put 'em up
And keep 'em up, when I could use my hands
For better things, for instance, counting pickles.
For such is man. He'll never put aside
His hardware of his own free will, say
For love of virtue, or to earn the praises
Of certain silver tongues at City Hall.
If I don't shoot, the other fellow will.
That's logic. Okay. And maybe now you'll ask:
What's to be done? I'll tell you. But first get
This straight: What you've been doing so far is
Disastrous: Sitting idly at your counters
Hoping that everything will be all right
And meanwhile disunited, bickering
Among yourselves, instead of mustering
A strong defence force that would shield you from
The gangsters' depredations. No, I say

This can't go on. The first thing that's needed
Is unity. The second is sacrifices.
What sacrifices? you may ask. Are we
To part with thirty cents on every dollar
For mere protection? No, nothing doing.
Our money is too precious. If protection
Were free of charge, then yes, we'd be all for it.
Well, my dear vegetable dealers, things
Are not so simple. Only death is free:
Everything else costs money. And that includes
Protection, peace and quiet. Life is like
That, and because it never will be any different
These gentlemen and I (there are more outside)
Have resolved to offer you protection.
Givola and Roma applaud.

But

To show you that we mean to operate
On solid business principles, we've asked
Our partner, Mr Clark here, the wholesaler
Whom you all know, to come here and address you.
*Roma pulls Clark forward. A few of the vegetable dealers
applaud.*

GIVOLA: Mr Clark, I bid you welcome in the name
Of this assembly. Mr Ui is honoured
To see the Cauliflower Trust supporting his
Initiative. I thank you, Mr Clark.

CLARK: We of the Cauliflower Trust observe
Ladies and gentlemen, with consternation
How hard it's getting for you vegetable
Dealers to sell your wares. 'Because,' I hear
You say, 'they're too expensive.' Yes, but why
Are they expensive? It's because our packers
And teamsters, pushed by outside agitators
Want more and more. And that's what Mr Ui
And Mr Ui's friends will put an end to.

FIRST DEALER: But if the little man gets less and less
     How is he going to buy our vegetables?
UI: Your question is a good one. Here's my answer:
     Like it or not, this modern world of ours
     Is inconceivable without the working man
     If only as a customer. I've always
     Insisted that honest work is no disgrace.
     Far from it. It's constructive and conducive
     To profits. As an individual
     The working man has all my sympathy.
     It's only when he bands together, when he
     Presumes to meddle in affairs beyond
     His understanding, such as profits, wages
     Etcetera, that I say: Watch your step
     Brother, a worker is somebody who works.
     But when you strike, when you stop working, then
     You're not a worker any more. Then you're
     A menace to society. And that's
     Where I step in.
Clark applauds.
                    However, to convince you
     That everything is open and above
     Board, let me call your attention to the presence
     Here of a man well-known, I trust, to
     Everybody here for his sterling honesty
     And incorruptible morality.
     His name is Dogsborough.
The vegetable dealers applaud a little louder.
                         Mr Dogsborough
     I owe you an incomparable debt
     Of gratitude. Our meeting was the work
     Of Providence. I never will forget –
     Not if I live to be a hundred – how
     You took me to your arms, an unassuming
     Son of the Bronx and chose me for your friend
     Nay more, your son.

He seizes Dogsborough's limply dangling hand and shakes it.

GIVOLA, *in an undertone*: How touching! Father and Son!

GIRI, *steps forward*:
Well, folks, the boss has spoken for us all.
I see some questions written on your faces.
Ask them! Don't worry. We won't eat you. You
Play square with us and we'll play square with you.
But get this straight: we haven't got much patience
With idle talk, especially the kind
That carps and cavils and finds fault
With everything. You'll find us open, though
To any healthy, positive suggestion
On ways and means of doing what must be done.
So fire away!
The vegetable dealers don't breathe a word.

GIVOLA, *unctuously*: And no holds barred. I think
You know me and my little flower shop.

A BODYGUARD: Hurrah for Givola!

GIVOLA: Okay, then. Do
You want protection? Or would you rather have
Murder, extortion and highway robbery?

FIRST DEALER: Things have been pretty quiet lately. I
Haven't had any trouble in my store.

SECOND DEALER: Nothing's wrong in my place.

THIRD DEALER: Nor in mine.

GIVOLA: That's odd.

SECOND DEALER: We've heard that recently in bars
Things have been happening just like Mr Ui
Was telling us, that glasses have been smashed
And gin poured down the drain in places that
Refused to cough up for protection. But
Things have been peaceful in the greengoods business.
So far at least, thank God.

ROMA: And what about
Sheet's murder? And Bowl's death? Is that
What you call peaceful?

SECOND DEALER: But is that connected
  With cauliflower, Mr Roma?
ROMA: No. Just a minute.
  *Roma goes over to Ui, who after his big speech has been sitting
  there exhausted and listless. After a few words he motions to
  Giri to join them. Givola also takes part in a hurried whispered
  conversation. Then Giri motions to one of the bodyguards and
  goes out quickly with him.*
GIVOLA: Friends, I've been asked to tell you that a poor
  Unhappy woman wishes to express
  Her thanks to Mr Ui in your presence.
  *He goes to the rear and leads in a heavily made-up and flashily
  dressed woman – Dockdaisy – who is holding a little girl by the
  hand. The three stop in front of Ui, who has stood up.*
GIVOLA: Speak, Mrs Bowl.
  To the vegetable dealers.
                    It's Mrs Bowl, the young
  Widow of Mr Bowl, the late accountant
  Of the Cauliflower Trust, who yesterday
  While on his way to City Hall to do
  His duty, was struck down by hand unknown.
  Mrs Bowl!
DOCKDAISY: Mr Ui, in my profound bereavement over my
  husband who was foully murdered while on his way to
  City Hall in the exercise of his civic duty, I wish to express
  my heartfelt thanks for the flowers you sent me and my
  little girl, aged six, who has been robbed of her father.
  To the vegetable dealers. Gentlemen, I'm only a poor widow
  and all I have to say is that without Mr Ui I'd be out in
  the street as I shall gladly testify at any time. My little girl,
  aged five, and I will never forget it, Mr Ui.
  Ui gives Dockdaisy his hand and chucks the child under the chin.
GIVOLA: Bravo!
  *Giri wearing Bowl's hat cuts through the crowd, followed by
  several gangsters carrying large gasoline cans. They make their
  way to the exit.*

UI: Mrs Bowl, my sympathies. This lawlessness
   This crime wave's got to stop because . . .

GIVOLA, *as the dealers start leaving*:   Hold it!
   The meeting isn't over. The next item
   Will be a song in memory of poor Bowl
   Sung by our friend James Greenwool, followed by
   A collection for the widow. He's a baritone.
   *One of the bodyguards steps forward and sings a sentimental song
   in which the word 'home' occurs frequently. During the performance the gangsters sit rapt, their heads in their hands, or leaning
   back with eyes closed, etc. The meagre applause at the end is
   interrupted by the howling of police and fire sirens. A red glow
   is seen in a large window in the background.*

ROMA: Fire on the waterfront!

A VOICE: Where?

A BODYGUARD *entering*:   Is there a vegetable
   Dealer named Hook in the house?

SECOND DEALER: That's me. What's wrong?

THE BODYGUARD: Your warehouse is on fire.
   *Hook, the dealer, rushes out. A few follow him. Others go to the
   window.*

ROMA: Hold it!
   Nobody leave the room!
   To the bodyguard.
                         Is it arson?

THE BODYGUARD: It must be. They've found some gasoline
   cans.

THIRD DEALER: Some gasoline cans were taken out of here!

ROMA, *in a rage*: What's that? Is somebody insinuating
   We did it?

A BODYGUARD, *pokes his automatic into the man's ribs*:
                   What was being taken out
   Of here? Did you see any gasoline cans?

OTHER BODYGUARDS, *to other dealers*:
   Did you see any cans? – Did you?

THE DEALERS: Not I . . .
  Me neither.
ROMA: That's better.
GIVOLA, *quickly*:   Ha. The very man
  Who just a while ago was telling us
  That all was quiet on the green goods front
  Now sees his warehouse burning, turned to ashes
  By malefactors. Don't you see? Can you
  Be blind? You've got to get together. And quick!
UI, *bellowing*: Things in this town are looking very sick!
  First murder and now arson! This should show
  You men that no one's safe from the next blow!
  A sign appears.

8

*The warehouse fire trial. Press. Judge. Prosecutor. Defence counsel.
Young Dogsborough. Giri. Givola. Dockdaisy. Bodyguards.
Vegetable dealers and Fish, the accused.*

a

*Emanuele Giri stands in front of the witness's chair, pointing at
Fish, the accused, who is sitting in utter apathy.*

GIRI, *shouting*: There sits the criminal who lit the fire!
  When I challenged him he was slinking down the street
  Clutching a gasoline can to his chest.
  Stand up, you bastard, when I'm talking to you.
  Fish is pulled to his feet. He stands swaying.
THE JUDGE: Defendant, pull yourself together. This is a

court of law. You are on trial for arson. That is a very serious matter, and don't forget it!

FISH, *in a thick voice*: Arlarlarl.

THE JUDGE: Where did you get that gasoline can?

FISH: Arlarl.

At a sign from the judge an excessively well-dressed, sinister-looking doctor bends down over Fish and exchanges glances with Giri.

THE DOCTOR: Simulating.

DEFENCE COUNSEL: The defence moves that other doctors be consulted.

THE JUDGE, *smiling*: Denied.

DEFENCE COUNSEL: Mr Giri, how did you happen to be on the spot when this fire, which reduced twenty-two buildings to ashes, broke out in Mr Hook's warehouse?

GIRI: I was taking a walk for my digestion.

Some of the bodyguards laugh. Giri joins in the laughter.

DEFENCE COUNSEL: Are you aware, Mr Giri, that Mr Fish, the defendant, is an unemployed worker, that he had never been in Chicago before and arrived here on foot the day before the fire?

GIRI: What? When?

DEFENCE COUNSEL: Is the registration number of your car XXXXXX?

GIRI: Yes.

DEFENCE COUNSEL: Was this car parked outside Dogsborough's restaurant on 87th Street during the four hours preceding the fire, and was defendant Fish dragged out of that restaurant in a state of unconsciousness?

GIRI: How should I know? I spent the whole day on a little excursion to Cicero, where I met fifty-two persons who are all ready to testify that they saw me.

The bodyguards laugh.

DEFENCE COUNSEL: Your previous statement left me with the impression that you were taking a walk for your digestion in the Chicago waterfront area.

GIRI: Any objection to my eating in Cicero and digesting
in Chicago?
*Loud and prolonged laughter in which the judge joins. Darkness.
An organ plays Chopin's* Funeral March *in dance rhythm.*

b

*When the lights go on, Hook, the vegetable dealer, is sitting in
the witness's chair.*

DEFENCE COUNSEL: Did you ever quarrel with the defend-
ant, Mr Hook? Did you ever see him before?
HOOK: Never.
DEFENCE COUNSEL: Have you ever seen Mr Giri?
HOOK: Yes. In the office of the Cauliflower Trust on the day
of the fire.
DEFENCE COUNSEL: Before the fire?
HOOK: Just before the fire. He passed through the room
with four men carrying gasoline cans.
Commotion on the press bench and among the bodyguards.
THE JUDGE: Would the gentlemen of the press please be
quiet.
DEFENCE COUNSEL: What premises does your warehouse
adjoin, Mr Hook?
HOOK: The premises of the former Sheet shipyard. There's
a passage connecting my warehouse with the shipyard.
DEFENCE COUNSEL: Are you aware, Mr Hook, that Mr
Giri lives in the former Sheet shipyard and consequently
has access to the premises?
HOOK: Yes. He's the stockroom superintendent.
*Increased commotion on the press bench. The bodyguards boo and
take a menacing attitude toward Hook, the defence and the press.
Young Dogsborough rushes up to the judge and whispers something
in his ear.*

JUDGE: Order in the court! The defendant is unwell. The court is adjourned.

Darkness. The organ starts again to play Chopin's Funeral March *in dance rhythm.*

c

When the lights go on, Hook is sitting in the witness's chair. He is in a state of collapse, with a cane beside him and bandages over his head and eyes.

THE PROSECUTOR: Is your eyesight poor, Hook?

HOOK, *with difficulty*: Yes.

THE PROSECUTOR: Would you say you were capable of recognising anyone clearly and definitely?

HOOK: No.

THE PROSECUTOR: Do you, for instance, recognise this man?

He points at Giri.

HOOK: No.

THE PROSECUTOR: You're not prepared to say that you ever saw him before?

HOOK: No.

THE PROSECUTOR: And now, Hook, a very important question. Think well before you answer. Does your warehouse adjoin the premises of the former Sheet shipyard?

HOOK, *after a pause*: No.

THE PROSECUTOR: That is all.

Darkness. The organ starts playing again.

d

When the lights go on, Dockdaisy is sitting in the witness's chair.

DOCKDAISY, *mechanically*: I recognise the defendant perfectly because of his guilty look and because he is five feet eight inches tall. My sister-in-law has informed me that he was seen outside City Hall on the afternoon my husband was shot while entering City Hall. He was carrying a Webster sub-machine gun and made a suspicious impression.
Darkness. The organ starts playing again.

e

When the lights go on, Giuseppe Givola is sitting in the witness's chair. Greenwool, the bodyguard, is standing near him.

THE PROSECUTOR: It has been alleged that certain men were seen carrying gasoline cans out of the offices of the Cauliflower Trust before the fire. What do you know about this?
GIVOLA: It couldn't be anybody but Mr Greenwool.
THE PROSECUTOR: Is Mr Greenwool in your employ?
GOVOLA: Yes.
THE PROSECUTOR: What is your profession, Mr Givola?
GIVOLA: Florist.
THE PROSECUTOR: Do florists use large quantities of gasoline?
GIVOLA, *seriously*: No, only for plant lice.

THE PROSECUTOR: What was Mr Greenwool doing in the
    offices of the Cauliflower Trust?
GIVOLA: Singing a song.
THE PROSECUTOR: Then he can't very well have carried
    any gasoline cans to Hook's warehouse at the same time.
GIVOLA: It's out of the question. It's not in his character to
    start fires. He's a baritone.
THE PROSECUTOR: If it please the court, I should like
    witness Greenwool to sing the fine song he was singing
    in the offices of the Cauliflower Trust while the warehouse
    was being set on fire.
THE JUDGE: The court does not consider it necessary.
GIVOLA: I protest.
He rises.
The bias in this courtroom is outrageous.
Cleancut young fellows who in broadest daylight
Fire a well-meant shot or two are treated
Like shady characters. It's scandalous.
Laughter. Darkness. The organ starts playing again.

f

*When the lights go on, the courtroom shows every indication of utter
exhaustion.*

THE JUDGE: The press has dropped hints that this court
    might be subject to pressure from certain quarters. The
    court wishes to state that it has been subjected to no
    pressure of any kind and is conducting this trial in perfect
    freedom. I believe this will suffice.
THE PROSECUTOR: Your Honour! In view of the fact that
    defendant Fish persists in simulating dementia, the
    prosecution holds that he cannot be questioned any
    further. We therefore move . . .

DEFENCE COUNSEL: Your honour. The defendant is coming to!
Commotion.

FISH, *seems to be waking up*: Arlarlwaratarlawatrla.

DEFENCE COUNSEL: Water! Your Honour! I ask leave to question defendant Fish.

Uproar.

THE PROSECUTOR: I object. I see no indication that Fish is in his right mind. It's all a machination on the part of the defence, cheap sensationalism, demagogy!

FISH: Watr.

Supported by the defence counsel, he stands up.

DEFENCE COUNSEL: Fish. Can you answer me?

FISH: Yarl.

DEFENCE COUNSEL: Fish, tell the court: Did you, on the 28th of last month, set fire to a vegetable warehouse on the waterfront? Yes or no?

FISH: N-n-no.

DEFENCE COUNSEL: When did you arrive in Chicago, Fish?

FISH: Water.

DEFENCE COUNSEL: Water!
Commotion. Young Dogsborough has stepped up to the judge and is talking to him emphatically.

GIRI *stands up square-shouldered and bellows*: Frame-up! Lies! Lies!

DEFENCE COUNSEL: Did you ever see this man – *He indicates Giri.* – before?

FISH: Yes. Water.

DEFENCE COUNSEL: Where? Was it in Dogsborough's restaurant on the waterfront?

FISH, *faintly*: Yes.
Uproar. The bodyguards draw their guns and boo. The doctor comes running in with a glass. He pours the contents into Fish's mouth before the defence counsel can take the glass out of his hand.

DEFENCE COUNSEL: I object. I move that this glass be examined.

THE JUDGE, *exchanging glances with the prosecutor*: Motion denied.

DOCKDAISY *screams at Fish*: Murderer!

DEFENCE COUNSEL: Your Honour!
Because the mouth of truth cannot be stopped with earth
They're trying to stop it with a piece of paper
A sentence to be handed down as though
Your Honour – that's their hope – should properly
Be titled Your Disgrace. They cry to justice:
Hands up! Is this our city, which has aged
A hundred years in seven days beneath
The onslaught of a small but bloody brood
Of monsters, now to see its justice murdered
Nay, worse than murdered, desecrated by
Submission to brute force? Your Honour!
Suspend this trial!

THE PROSECUTOR: I object!

GIRI: You dog!
You lying, peculating dog! Yourself
A poisoner! Come on! Let's step outside!
I'll rip your guts out! Gangster!

DEFENCE COUNSEL: The whole
Town knows this man.

GIRI, *fuming*:   Shut up!
When the judge tries to interrupt him:
                                You too!
Just keep your trap shut if you want to live!
He runs short of breath and the judge manages to speak.

THE JUDGE: Order in the court. Defence counsel will incur charges of contempt of court. Mr Giri's indignation is quite understandable. *To the defence counsel*: Continue.

DEFENCE COUNSEL: Fish! Did they give you anything to drink at Dogsborough's restaurant? Fish! Fish!

GIEI, *bellowing*: Go on and shout! Looks like his tyre's gone
  down.
  We'll see who's running things in this here town!
  *Uproar. Darkness. The organ starts again to play Chopin's
  Funeral March in dance rhythm.*

g

*As the lights go on for the last time, the judge stands up and in a
toneless voice delivers the sentence. The defendant is deathly pale.*

THE JUDGE: Charles Fish, I find you guilty of arson and
  sentence you to fifteen years at hard labour.
  A sign appears.

9

a

*Cicero. A woman climbs out of a shot-up truck and staggers
forward.*

THE WOMAN: Help! Help! Don't run away. Who'll testify?
  My husband is in that truck. They got him. Help!
  My arm is smashed . . . And so's the truck. I need
  A bandage for my arm. They gun us down
  Like rabbits. God! Won't anybody help?
  You murderers! My husband! I know who's
  Behind it. Ui! *Raging*: Fiend! Monster! Shit!
  You'd make an honest piece of shit cry out:
  Where can I wash myself? You lousy louse!
  And people stand for it. And we go under.

Hey you! It's Ui!
A burst of machine-gun fire nearby. She collapses.
                    Ui did this job!
Where's everybody? Help! who'll stop that mob?

b

Dogsborough's country house. Night toward morning.
Dogsborough is writing his will and confession.

DOGSBOROUGH:
   And so I, honest Dogsborough acquiesced
   In all the machinations of that bloody gang
   After full eighty years of uprightness.
   I'm told that those who've known me all along
   Are saying I don't know what's going on
   That if I knew I wouldn't stand for it.
   Alas, I know it all. I know who set
   Fire to Hook's warehouse. And I know who dragged
   Poor Fish into the restaurant and doped him.
   I know that when Sheet died a bloody death
   His steamship ticket in his pocket, Roma
   Was there. I know that Giri murdered Bowl
   That afternoon outside of City Hall
   Because he knew too much about myself
   Honest old Dogsborough. I know that he
   Shot Hook, and saw him with Hook's hat.
   I know that Givola committed five
   Murders, here itemised. I also know
   All about Ui, and I know he knew
   All this – the deaths of Sheet and Bowl, Givola's
   Murderers and all about the fire. All this
   Your honest Dogsborough knew. All this
   He tolerated out of sordid lust
   For gain, and fear of forfeiting your trust.

10

*Hotel Mammoth. Ui's suite. Ui is sitting slumped in a deep chair,
staring into space. Givola is writing and two bodyguards are looking
over his shoulder, grinning.*

GIVOLA: And so I, Dogsborough, bequeath my bar
  To good hard-working Givola. My country
  House to the brave, though somewhat hot-headed Giri.
  And I bequeath my son to honest Roma.
  I furthermore request that you appoint
  Roma police chief, Giri judge, and Givola
  Commissioner of welfare. For my own
  Position I would warmly recommend
  Arturo Ui, who, believe your honest
  Old Dogsborough, is worthy of it. – That's
  Enough, I think, let's hope he kicks in soon.
  This testament will do wonders. Now that the old
  Man's known to be dying and the hope arises
  Of laying him to rest with relative
  Dignity, in clean earth, it's well to tidy up
  His corpse. A pretty epitaph is needed.
  Ravens from olden time have battened on
  The reputation of the fabulous
  White raven that somebody saw sometime
  And somewhere. This old codger's their white raven.
  I guess they couldn't find a whiter one.
  And by the way, boss, Giri for my taste
  Is too much with him. I don't like it.

UI, *starting up*:   Giri?
  What about Giri?

GIVOLA: Only that he's spending
  A little too much time with Dogsborough.
UI: I
  Don't trust him.
  Giri comes in wearing a new hat, Hook's.
GIVOLA: I don't either. Hi, Giri
  How's Dogsborough's apoplexy?
GIRI: He refuses
  To let the doctor in.
GIVOLA: Our brilliant doctor
  Who took such loving care of Fish?
GIRI: No other
  Will do. The old man talks too much.
UI: Maybe somebody's talked too much to him . . .
GIRI: What's that? *To Givola*: You skunk, have you been
    stinking up
  The air around here again?
GIVOLA, *alarmed*: ·   Just read the will
  Dear Giri.
GIRI, *snatches it from him*:
                What! Police chief? Him? Roma?
  You must be crazy.
GIVOLA: He demands it. I'm
  Against it too. The bastard can't be trusted
  Across the street.
  Roma comes in followed by bodyguards.
                    Hi, Roma. Take a look at
  This will.
ROMA, *grabbing it out of his hands*:
                Okay, let's see it. What do you know!
  Giri a judge! But where's the old man's scribble?
GIRI: Under his pillow. He's been trying to
  Smuggle it out. Five times I've caught his son.
ROMA *holds out his hand*:
  Let's have it, Giri.
GIRI: What? I haven't got it.

ROMA: Oh yes, you have!
They glare at each other furiously.

                              I know what's on your mind.
There's something about Sheet. That concerns me.
GIRI: Bowl figures in it too. That concerns *me*.
ROMA: Okay, but you're both jerks, and I'm a man.
I know you, Giri, and you too, Givola.
I'd even say your crippled leg was phony.
Why do I always find you bastards here?
What are you cooking up? What lies have they
Been telling you about me, Arturo? Watch
Your step, you pipsqueaks. If I catch you trying
To cross me up, I'll rub you out like blood spots.
GIRI: Roma, you'd better watch your tongue. I'm not
One of your two-bit gunmen.
ROMA, *to his bodyguards*:   That means you!
That's what they're calling you at headquarters.
They hobnob with the Cauliflower Trust –
Pointing to Giri.
That shirt was made to order by Clark's tailor –
You two-bit gunmen do the dirty work –
And you – *To Ui.* – put up with it.
UI, *as though waking up*:   Put up with what?
GIVOLA: His shooting up Caruther's trucks. Caruther's
A member of the Trust.
UI: Did you shoot up
Caruther's trucks?
ROMA: I gave no orders. Just
Some of the boys. Spontaneous combustion.
They don't see why it's always the small grocers
That have to sweat and bleed. Why not the big wheels?
Damn it, Arturo, I myself don't get it.
GIVOLA: The Trust is good and mad.
GIRI: Clark says they're only
Waiting for it to happen one more time.
He's put in a complaint with Dogsborough.

UI, *morosely*: Ernesto, these things mustn't happen.

GIRI: Crack down, boss!
These guys are getting too big for their breeches.

GIVOLA: The Trust is good and mad, boss.

ROMA *pulls his gun. To Giri and Givola*:
Okay. Hands up!
To their bodyguards:
                         You too!
Hands up the lot of you. No monkey business!
Now back up to the wall.
*Givola, his men, and Giri raise their hands and with an air of
resignation back up to the wall.*

UI, *indifferently*:   What is all this?
Ernesto, don't make them nervous. What are you guys
Squabbling about? So some palooka's wasted
Some bullets on a cauliflower truck.
Such misunderstandings can be straightened out.
Everything is running smooth as silk.
The fire was a big success. The stores
Are paying for protection. Thirty cents
On every dollar. Almost half the city
Has knuckled under in five days. Nobody
Raises a hand against us. And I've got
Bigger and better projects.

GIVOLA, *quickly*:   Projects? What
For instance?

GIRI: Fuck your projects. Get this fool
To let me put my hands down.

ROMA: Safety first, Arturo.
We'd better leave them up.

GIVOLA: Won't it look sweet
If Clark comes in and sees us here like this?

UI: Ernesto, put that rod away!

ROMA: No dice!
Wake up, Arturo. Don't you see their game?
They're selling you out to the Clarks and Dogsboroughs.

'If Clark comes in and sees us!' What, I ask you
Has happened to the shipyard's funds? We haven't
Seen a red cent. The boys shoot up the stores
Tote gasoline to warehouses and sigh:
We made Arturo what he is today
And he doesn't know us any more. He's playing
The shipyard owner and tycoon. Wake up
Arturo!

GIRI: Right. And speak up. Tell us where
You stand.

UI *jumps up*:   Are you boys trying to pressure me
At gunpoint? Better not, I'm warning you
You won't get anywhere with me like that.
You'll only have yourselves to blame for
The consequences. I'm a quiet man. But
I won't be threatened. Either trust me blindly
Or go your way. I owe you no accounting.
Just do your duty, and do it to the full.
The recompense is up to me, because
Duty comes first and then the recompense.
What I demand of you is trust. You lack
Faith, and where faith is lacking, all is lost.
How do you think I got this far? By faith!
Because of my fanatical, my unflinching
Faith in the cause. With faith and nothing else
I flung a challenge at this city and forced
It to its knees. With faith I made my way
To Dogsborough. With faith I climbed the steps
Of City Hall. With nothing in my naked
Hands but indomitable faith.

ROMA: And
A tommy gun.

UI: No, other men have them
But lack firm faith in their predestination
To leadership. And that is why you too
Need to have faith in me. Have faith! Believe that

I know what's best for you and that I'm
Resolved to put it through. That I will find
The road to victory. If Dogsborough
Passes away, then I decide who gets to
Be what. I say no more, but rest assured:
You'll all be satisfied.

GIVOLA *puts his hand on his heart*:

Arturo!

ROMA, *sullenly*:   Scram
You guys!
*Giri, Givola and Givola's bodyguard go out slowly with their
hands up.*

GIRI, *leaving, to Roma*: I like your hat.

GIVOLA, *leaving*:   Dear Roma . . .

ROMA: Scram!
Giri, you clown, don't leave your laugh behind.
And Givola, you crook, be sure to take
Your clubfoot, though I'm pretty sure you stole it.
When they are gone, Ui relapses into his brooding.

UI: I want to be alone.

ROMA, *standing still*:   Arturo, if I
Hadn't the kind of faith you've just described
I'd sometimes find it hard to look my
Men in the face. We've got to act. And quickly.
Giri is cooking up some dirty work.

UI: Don't worry about Giri. I am planning
Bigger and better things. And now, Ernesto
To you, my oldest friend and trusted lieutenant
I will divulge them.

ROMA, *beaming*:   Speak, Arturo. Giri
And what I had to say of him can wait.
He sits down with Ui. Roma's men stand waiting in the corner.

UI: We're finished with Chicago. I need more.

ROMA: More?

UI: Vegetables are sold in other cities.

ROMA: But how are you expecting to get in?

UI: Through
   The front door, through the back door, through the
      windows.
   Resisted, sent away, called back again.
   Booed and acclaimed. With threats and supplications
   Appeals and insults, gentle force and steel
   Embrace. In short, the same as here.
ROMA: Except
   Conditions aren't the same in other places.
UI: I have in mind a kind of dress rehearsal
   In a small town. That way we'll see
   Whether conditions are so different. I
   Doubt it.
ROMA: And where have you resolved to stage
   This dress rehearsal?
UI: In Cicero.
ROMA: But there
   They've got this Dullfeet with his Journal
   For Vegetables and Positive Thinking
   Which every Saturday accuses me
   Of murdering Sheet.
UI: That's got to stop.
ROMA: It will. These journalists have enemies.
   Their black and white makes certain people
   See red. Myself, for instance. Yes, Arturo
   I think these accusations can be silenced.
UI: I'm sure they can. The Trust is negotiating
   With Cicero right now. For the time being
   We'll just sell cauliflower peacefully.
ROMA: Who's doing this negotiating?
UI: Clark.
   But he's been having trouble. On our account.
ROMA: I see. So Clark is in it. I wouldn't trust
   That Clark around the corner.
UI: In Cicero
   They say we're following the Cauliflower

Trust like its shadow. They want cauliflower, but
They don't want us. The shopkeepers don't like us.
A feeling shared by others: Dullfeet's wife
For instance, who for years now has been running
A greengoods wholesale house. She'd like to join
The Trust, and would have joined except for us.

ROMA: You mean this plan of moving in on Cicero
Didn't start with you at all, but with the Trust?
Arturo, now I see it all. I see
Their rotten game.

UI: Whose game?

ROMA: The Trust's.
The goings-on at Dogsborough's! His will!
It's all a machination of the Trust.
They want the Cicero connection. You're in
The way. But how can they get rid of you?
You've got them by the balls, because they needed
You for their dirty business and connived at
Your methods. But now they've found a way:
Old Dogsborough confesses and repairs
In ash and sackcloth to his coffin.
The cauliflower boys with deep emotion
Retrieve this paper from his hands and sobbing
Read it to the assembled press: how he repents
And solemnly adjures them to wipe out
The plague which he – as he confesses – brought
In, and restore the cauliflower trade
To its time-honoured practices.
That's what they plan, Arturo. They're all in it:
Giri, who gets Dogsborough to scribble wills
And who is hand in glove with Clark, who's having
Trouble in Cicero because of us
And wants pure sunshine when he shovels shekels.
Givola, who smells carrion. – This Dogsborough
Honest old Dogsborough with his two-timing will
That splatters you with muck has got to be

Rubbed out, Arturo, or your best-laid plans
For Cicero are down the drain.

UI: You think
It's all a plot? It's true. They've kept me out
Of Cicero. I've noticed that.

ROMA: Arturo
I beg you: let me handle this affair.
I tell you what: my boys and I will beat
It out to Dogsborough's tonight
And take him with us. To the hospital
We'll tell him – and deliver him to the morgue.

UI: But Giri's with him at the villa.

ROMA: He
Can stay there.
They exchange glances.
                    Two birds one stone.

UI: And Givola?

ROMA: On the way back I'll drop in at the florist's
And order handsome wreaths for Dogsborough.
For Giri too, the clown. And I'll pay cash.
He pats his gun.

UI: Ernesto, this contemptible project of
The Dogsboroughs and Clarks and Dullfeets
To squeeze me out of Cicero's affairs
By coldly branding me a criminal
Must be frustrated with an iron hand.
I put my trust in you.

ROMA: And well you may.
But you must meet with us before we start
And give the boys a talk to make them see
The matter in its proper light. I'm not
So good at talking.

UI, *shaking his hand*: It's a deal.

ROMA: I knew it
Arturo. This was how it had to be
Decided. Say, the two of us! Say, you

And me! Like in the good old days.
To his men.

What did
I tell you, boys? He gives us the green light.
UI: I'll be there.
ROMA: At eleven.
UI: Where?
ROMA: At the garage.
   I'm a new man. At last we'll see some fight!
   He goes out quickly with his men. Pacing the floor, Ui prepares
   the speech he is going to make to Roma's men.
UI: Friends, much as I regret to say it, word
   Has reached me that behind my back perfidious
   Treason is being planned. Men close to me
   Men whom I trusted implicitly
   Have turned against me. Goaded by ambition
   And crazed by lust for gain, these despicable
   Fiends have conspired with the cauliflower
   Moguls – no, that won't do – with who? I've got it!
   With the police, to coldly liquidate you
   And even, so I hear, myself. My patience
   Is at an end. I therefore order you
   Under Ernesto Roma who enjoys
   My fullest confidence, tonight . . .
   Enter Clark, Giri and Betty Dullfeet.
GIRI, *noticing that Ui looks frightened*: It's only
   Us, boss.
CLARK: Ui, let me introduce
   Mrs Dullfeet of Cicero. The Trust
   Asks you to give her your attention, and hopes
   The two of you will come to terms.
UI, *scowling*:   I'm listening.
CLARK: A merger, as you know, is being considered
   Between Chicago's Cauliflower Trust
   And Cicero's purveyors. In the course
   Of the negotiations, Cicero

Objected to your presence on the board.
The Trust was able, after some discussion
To overcome this opposition. Mrs Dullfeet
Is here . . .

MRS DULLFEET: To clear up the misunderstanding.
Moreover, I should like to point out that
My husband, Mr Dullfeet's newspaper
Campaign was not directed against you
Mr Ui.

UI: Against who was it directed?

CLARK: I may as well speak plainly, Ui. Sheet's
'Suicide' made a very bad impression
In Cicero. Whatever else Sheet may
Have been, he was a shipyard owner
A leading citizen, and not some Tom
Dick or Harry whose death arouses no
Comment. And something else. Caruther's
Garage complains of an attack on one of
Its trucks. And one of your men, Ui, is
Involved in both these cases.

MRS DULLFEET: Every child in
Cicero knows Chicago's cauliflower
Is stained with blood.

UI: Have you come here to insult me?

MRS DULLFEET:
No, no. Not you, since Mr Clark has vouched
For you. It's this man Roma.

CLARK, *quickly*:   Cool it, Ui!

GIRI: Cicero . . .

UI: You can't talk to me like this!
What do you take me for? I've heard enough!
Ernesto Roma is my man. I don't
Let anybody tell me who to pal with.
This is an outrage.

GIRI: Boss!

MRS DULLFEET: Ignatius Dullfeet

Will fight the Romas of this world to his
Last breath.

CLARK, *coldly*: And rightly so. In that the Trust
Is solidly behind him. Think it over.
Friendship and business are two separate things.
What do you say?

UI, *likewise coldly*:   You heard me, Mr Clark.

CLARK: Mrs Dullfeet, I regret profoundly
The outcome of this interview.
On his way out, to Ui:

Most unwise, Ui.
Left alone, Ui and Giri do not look at each other.   .

GIRI: This and the business with Caruther's truck
Means war. That's plain.

UI: I'm not afraid of war.

GIRI: Okay, you're not afraid. You'll only have
The Trust, the papers, the whole city, plus
Dogsborough and his crowd against you.
Just between you and me, boss, I'd think twice . . .

UI: I know my duty and need no advice.
A sign appears.

II

*Garage. Night. The sound of rain. Ernesto Roma and young Inna.
In the background gunmen.*

INNA: It's one o'clock.

ROMA: He must have been delayed.

INNA: Could he be hesitating?

ROMA: He could be.
Arturo's so devoted to his henchmen
He'd rather sacrifice himself than them.
Even with rats like Givola and Giri

He can't make up his mind. And so he dawdles
And wrestles with himself. It might be two
Or even three before he gets a move on.
But never fear, he'll come. Of course he will.
I know him, Inna.
Pause.

                  When I see that Giri
Flat on the carpet, pouring out his guts
I'll feel as if I'd taken a good leak.
Oh well, it won't be long.

INNA: These rainy nights are
Hard on the nerves.

ROMA: That's what I like about them.
Of nights the blackest
Of cars the fastest
And of friends
The most resolute.

INNA: .   How many years have
You known him?

ROMA: Going on eighteen.

INNA: That's a long time.

A GUNMAN *comes forward*:
        The boys want whisky.

ROMA: No. Tonight I need
Them sober.
A little man is brought in by the bodyguards.

THE LITTLE MAN, *out of breath*:
        Dirty work at the crossroads!
Two armoured cars outside police H.Q.
Jam-packed with cops.

ROMA: Okay, boys, get the
Bullet-proof shutter down. Those cops have got
Nothing to do with us, but foresight's better
Than hindsight.
Slowly an iron shutter falls, blocking the garage door.
        Is the passage clear?

INNA *nods*: It's a funny thing about tobacco. When a man
　Is smoking, he looks calm. And if you imitate
　A calm-looking man and light a cigarette, you
　Get to be calm yourself.
ROMA, *smiling*:　　　　　　Hold out your hand.
INNA *does so*: It's trembling. That's no good.
ROMA:　　　　　　　　　　　　Don't worry. It's all
　Right. I don't go for bruisers. They're unfeeling.
　Nothing can hurt them and they won't hurt you.
　Not seriously. Tremble all you like.
　A compass needle is made of steel but trembles
　Before it settles on its course. Your hand
　Is looking for its pole. That's all.
A SHOUT, *from the side*:　　　　　Police car
　Coming down Church Street.
ROMA, *intently*:　　　　　Is it stopping?
THE VOICE:　　　　　　　　　　　No.
A GUNMAN *comes in*:
　Two cars with blacked-out lights have turned the corner.
ROMA: They're waiting for Arturo. Givola and
　Giri are laying for him. He'll run straight
　Into their trap. We've got to head him off.
　Let's go!
A GUNMAN: It's suicide.
ROMA:　　　　　　　If suicide it is
　Let it be suicide! Hell! Eighteen years
　Of friendship!
INNA, *loud and clear*: Raise the shutter!
　Machine-gun ready?
A GUNMAN:　　　　Ready.
INNA:　　　　　　　Up she goes.
　The bullet-proof shutter rises slowly. Ui and Givola enter briskly,
　followed by bodyguards.
ROMA: Arturo!
INNA, *under his breath*: Yeah, and Givola.
ROMA:　　　　　　　　　　　　What's up?

Arturo, man, you had us worried. *Laughs loudly.* Hell!
But everything's okay.

UI, *hoarsely:*   Why wouldn't it be okay?

INNA: We thought
Something was wrong. If I were you I'd give him
The glad-hand, boss. He was going to lead
Us all through fire to save you. Weren't you, Roma?
*Ui goes up to Roma, holding out his hand. Roma grasps it,
laughing. At this moment, when Roma cannot reach for his gun,
Givola shoots him from the hip.*

UI: Into the corner with them!
*Roma's men stand bewildered. Inna in the lead, they are driven
into the corner. Givola bends down over Roma, who is lying on the
floor.*

GIVOLA: He's still breathing.

UI: Finish him off.
To the men lined up against the wall.
Your vicious plot against me is exposed.
So are your plans to rub out Dogsborough.
I caught you in the nick of time. Resistance
Is useless. I'll teach you to rebel against me!
You bastards!

GIVOLA: Not a single one unarmed!
Speaking of Roma:
He's coming to. He's going to wish he hadn't.

UI: I'll be at Dogsborough's country house tonight.
He goes out quickly.

INNA: You stinking rats! You traitors!

GIVOLA, *excitedly:*   Let 'em have it!
*The men standing against the wall are mowed down by machine-
gun fire.*

ROMA *comes to:*
Givola! Christ.
Turns over, his face chalky-white.
                    What happened over there?

GIVOLA: Nothing. Some traitors have been executed.

ROMA: You dog! My men! What have you done to them?
Givola does not answer.
And where's Arturo? You've murdered him. I knew it!
Looking for him on the floor.
Where is he?
GIVOLA: He's just left.
ROMA, *as he is being dragged to the wall*: You stinking dogs!
GIVOLA, *coolly*: You say my leg is short, I say your brain is
   small.
Now let your pretty legs convey you to the wall!
A sign appears.

12

*Givola's flower shop. Ignatius Dullfeet, a very small man, and
Betty Dullfeet come in.*

DULLFEET: I don't like this at all.
BETTY: Why not? They've gotten rid
   Of Roma.
DULLFEET: Yes, they've murdered him.
BETTY: That's how
   They do it. Anyway, he's gone. Clark says
   That Ui's years of storm and stress, which even
   The best of men go through, are over. Ui
   Has shown he wants to mend his uncouth ways.
   But if you persevere in your attacks
   You'll only stir his evil instincts up
   Again, and you, Ignatius, will be first
   To bear the brunt. But if you keep your mouth shut
   They'll leave you be.
DULLFEET: I'm not so sure my silence
   Will help.

BETTY: It's sure to. They're not beasts.

Giri comes in from one side, wearing Roma's hat.

GIRI: Hi. Here already? Mr Ui's inside.
He'll be delighted. Sorry I can't stay.
I've got to beat it quick before I'm seen.
I've swiped a hat from Givola.

He laughs so hard that plaster falls from the ceiling, and goes out, waving.

DULLFEET:
Bad when they growl. No better when they laugh.

BETTY: Don't say such things, Ignatius. Not here.

DULLFEET, *bitterly*:   Nor
Anywhere else.

BETTY: What can you do? Already
The rumour's going around in Cicero
That Ui's stepping into Dogsborough's shoes.
And worse, the greengoods men of Cicero
Are flirting with the Cauliflower Trust.

DULLFEET:
And now they've smashed two printing presses on me.
Betty, I've got a dark foreboding.

Givola and Ui come in with outstretched hands.

BETTY: Hi, Ui!

UI: Welcome. Dullfeet!

DULLFEET: Mr Ui
I tell you frankly that I hesitated
To come, because . . .

UI: Why hesitate? A man
Like you is welcome everywhere.

GIVOLA: So is a
Beautiful woman.

DULLFEET: Mr Ui, I've felt
It now and then to be my duty to
Come out against . . .

UI: A mere misunderstanding!
If you and I had known each other from

The start, it never would have happened. It
Has always been my fervent wish that what
Had to be done should be done peacefully.

DULLFEET: Violence . . .

UI: No one hates it more than I do.
If men were wise, there'd be no need of it.

DULLFEET: My aim . . .

UI: Is just the same as mine. We both
Want trade to thrive. The small shopkeeper whose
Life is no bed of roses nowadays
Must be permitted to sell his greens in peace.
And find protection when attacked.

DULLFEET, *firmly*:   And be
Free to determine whether he desires
Protection. I regard that as essential.

UI: And so do I. He's *got* to be free to choose.
Why? Because when he chooses his protector
Freely, and puts his trust in somebody he himself
Has chosen, then the confidence, which is
As necessary in the greengoods trade
As anywhere else, will prevail. That's always been
My stand.

DULLFEET: I'm glad to hear it from your lips.
For, no offence intended, Cicero
Will never tolerate coercion.

UI: Of course not.
No one, unless he has to, tolerates
Coercion.

DULLFEET: Frankly, if this merger with the Trust
Should mean importing the ungodly bloodbath
That plagues Chicago to our peaceful town
I never could approve it.
Pause.

UI: Frankness calls
For frankness, Mr Dullfeet. Certain things
That might not meet the highest moral standards

May have occurred in the past. Such things
Occur in battle. Among friends, however
They cannot happen. Dullfeet, what I want
Of you is only that in the future you should
Trust me and look upon me as a friend
Who never till the seas run dry will forsake
A friend – and, to be more specific, that
Your paper should stop printing these horror stories
That only make bad blood. I don't believe
I'm asking very much.

DULLFEET: It's easy not
To write about what doesn't happen, sir.

UI: Exactly. And if now and then some trifling
Incident should occur, because the earth
Is inhabited by men and not by angels
You will abstain, I hope, from printing lurid
Stories about trigger-happy criminals.
I wouldn't go so far as to maintain that
One of our drivers might not on occasion
Utter an uncouth word. That too is human.
And if some vegetable dealer stands
One of our men to a beer for punctual
Delivery of his carrots, let's not rush
Into print with stories of corruption.

BETTY: Mr
Ui, my husband's human.

GIVOLA: We don't doubt it.
And now that everything has been so amiably
Discussed and settled among friends, perhaps
You'd like to see my flowers . . .

UI, *to Dullfeet*:   After you.

*They inspect Givola's flower shop. Ui leads Betty, Givola leads
Dullfeet. In the following they keep disappearing behind the
flower displays. Givola and Dullfeet emerge.*

GIVOLA: These, my dear Dullfeet, are Malayan fronds.

DULLFEET: Growing, I see, by little oval ponds.

GIVOLA: Stocked with blue carp that stay stock-still for
hours.

DULLFEET: The wicked are insensitive to flowers.

They disappear. Ui and Betty emerge.

BETTY: A strong man needs no force to win his suit.

UI: Arguments carry better when they shoot.

BETTY: Sound reasoning is bound to take effect.

UI: Except when one is trying to collect.

BETTY: Intimidation, underhanded tricks . . .

UI: I prefer to speak of pragmatic politics.

They disappear. Givola and Dullfeet emerge.

DULLFEET: Flowers are free from lust and wickedness.

GIVOLA: Exactly why I love them, I confess.

DULLFEET: They live so quietly. They never hurry.

GIVOLA, *mischievously*:

No problems. No newspapers. No worry.

They disappear. Ui and Betty emerge.

BETTY: They tell me you're as abstinent as a vicar.

UI: I never smoke and have no use for liquor.

BETTY: A saint perhaps when all is said and done.

UI: Of carnal inclinations I have none.

They disappear. Givola and Dullfeet emerge.

DULLFEET: Your life with flowers must deeply satisfy.

GIVOLA: It would, had I not other fish to fry.

They disappear. Ui and Betty emerge.

BETTY: What, Mr Ui, does religion mean to you?

UI: I am a Christian. That will have to do.

BETTY: Yes. But the Ten Commandments, where do they
Come in?

UI:　　　　　In daily life they don't, I'd say.

BETTY: Forgive me if your patience I abuse
But what exactly are your social views?

UI: My social views are balanced, clear and healthy.
What proves it is: I don't neglect the wealthy.

They disappear. Givola and Dullfeet emerge.

DULLFEET: The flowers have their life, their social calls.

GIVOLA: I'll say they do. Especially funerals!

DULLFEET: Oh, I forgot that flowers were your bread.

GIVOLA: Exactly. My best clients are the dead.

DULLFEET: I hope that's not your only source of trade.

GIVOLA: Some people have the sense to be afraid.

DULLFEET: Violence, Givola, brings no lasting glory.

GIVOLA: It gets results, though.

DULLFEET: That's another story.

GIVOLA: You look so pale.

DULLFEET: The air is damp and close.

GIVOLA: The heavy scent affects you, I suppose.

They disappear. Ui and Betty emerge.

BETTY: I am so glad you two have worked things out.

UI: Once frankness showed what it was all about . . .

BETTY: Foul-weather friends will never disappoint . . .

UI, *putting his arm around her shoulder*:

I like a woman who can get the point.

Givola and Dullfeet, who is deathly pale, emerge. Dullfeet sees the hand on his wife's shoulder.

DULLFEET: Betty, we're leaving.

UI *comes up to him, holding out his hand*:

                         Mr Dullfeet, your

Decision honours you. It will redound to

Cicero's welfare. A meeting between such men

As you and me can only be auspicious.

GIVOLA, *giving Betty flowers*:

Beauty to beauty!

BETTY: Look, how nice, Ignatius!

Oh, I'm so happy. 'Bye, 'bye.

GIVOLA: Now we can

Start going places.

UI, *darkly*:   I don't like that man.

A sign appears.

13

Bells. A coffin is being carried into the Cicero funeral chapel, followed by Betty Dullfeet in widow's weeds, and by Clark, Ui, Giri and Givola bearing enormous wreaths. After handing in their wreaths, Giri and Givola remain outside the chapel. The pastor's voice is heard from inside.

VOICE: And so Ignatius Dullfeet's mortal frame
 Is laid to rest. A life of meagrely
 Rewarded toil is ended, of toil devoted
 To others than the toiler who has left us.
 The angel at the gates of heaven will set
 His hand upon Ignatius Dullfeet's shoulder
 Feel that his cloak has been worn thin and say:
 This man has borne the burdens of his neighbours.
 And in the city council for some time
 To come, when everyone has finished speaking
 Silence will fall. For so accustomed are
 His fellow citizens to listen to
 Ignatius Dullfeet's voice that they will wait
 To hear him. 'Tis as though the city's conscience
 Had died. This man who met with so untimely
 An end could walk the narrow path unseeing.
 Justice was in his heart. This man of lowly
 Stature but lofty mind created in
 His newspaper a rostrum whence his voice
 Rang out beyond the confines of our city.
 Ignatius Dullfeet, rest in peace! Amen.
GIVOLA: A tactful man: no word of how he died.
GIRI, *wearing Dullfeet's hat*:
 A tactful man? A man with seven children.
 Clark and Mulberry come out of the chapel.

CLARK: God damn it! Are you mounting guard for fear
  The truth might be divulged beside his coffin?
GIVOLA: Why so uncivil, my dear Clark? I'd think
  This holy place would curb your temper. And
  Besides, the boss is out of sorts. He doesn't
  Like the surroundings here.
MULBERRY: You murderers!
  Ignatius Dullfeet kept his word – and silence.
GIVOLA: Silence is not enough. The kind of men
  We need must be prepared not only to
  Keep silent for us but to speak – and loudly.
MULBERRY: What could he say except to call you butchers?
GIVOLA: He had to go. That little Dullfeet was
  The pore through which the greengoods dealers oozed
  Cold sweat. He stank of it unbearably.
GIRI: And what about your cauliflower? Do
  You want it sold in Cicero or don't
  You?
MULBERRY: Not by slaughter.
GIRI: Hypocrite, how else?
  Who helps us eat the calf we slaughter, eh?
  You're funny bastards, clamouring for meat
  Then bawling out the cook because he uses
  A cleaver. We expect you guys to smack
  Your lips and all you do is gripe. And now
  Go home!
MULBERRY: A sorry day, Clark, when you brought
  These people in.
CLARK: You're telling me?
  The two go out, deep in gloom.
GIRI: Boss
  Don't let those stinkers keep you from enjoying
  The funeral!
GIVOLA: Pst! Betty's coming.
  Leaning on another woman, Betty comes out of the chapel.
  Ui steps up to her. Organ music from the chapel.

UI: Mrs
Dullfeet, my sympathies.
She passes him without a word.

GIRI, *bellowing*:   Hey, you!
She stops still and turns around. Her face is white.

UI: ..   I said, my
Sympathies, Mrs Dullfeet. Dullfeet – God
Have mercy on his soul – is dead. But cauliflower –
Your cauliflower – is still with us. Maybe you
Can't see it, because your eyes are still
Blinded with tears. This tragic incident
Should not, however, blind you to the fact
That shots are being fired from craven ambush
On law-abiding vegetable trucks.
And kerosene dispensed by ruthless hands
Is spoiling sorely needed vegetables.
My men and I stand ready to provide
Protection. What's your answer?

BETTY, *looking heavenward*:   This
With Dullfeet hardly settled in his grave!

UI: Believe me, I deplore the incident:
The man by ruthless hand extinguished was
My friend.

BETTY: The hand that felled him was the hand
That shook his hand in friendship. Yours!

UI: Am I
Never to hear the last of these foul rumours
This calumny which poisons at the root
My noblest aspirations and endeavours
To live in harmony with my fellow men?
Oh, why must they refuse to understand me?
Why will they not requite my trust? What malice
To speak of threats when I appeal to reason!
To spurn the hand that I hold out in friendship!

BETTY: You hold it out to murder.

UI: No!
  I plead with them and they revile me.
BETTY: You
  Plead like a serpent pleading with a bird.
UI: You've heard her. That's how people talk to me.
  It was the same with Dullfeet. He mistook
  My warm, my open-hearted offer of friendship
  For calculation and my generosity
  For weakness. How, alas, did he requite
  My friendly words? With stony silence. Silence
  Was his reply when what I hoped for
  Was joyful appreciation. Oh, how I longed to
  Hear him respond to my persistent, my
  Well-nigh humiliating pleas for friendship, or
  At least for a little understanding, with
  Some sign of human warmth. I longed in vain.
  My only reward was grim contempt. And even
  The promise to keep silent that he gave me
  So sullenly and God knows grudgingly
  Was broken on the first occasion. Where
  I ask you is this silence that he promised
  So fervently? New horror stories are being
  Broadcast in all directions. But I warn you:
  Don't go too far, for even my proverbial
  Patience has got its breaking point.
BETTY: Words fail me.
UI: Unprompted by the heart, they always fail.
BETTY: You call it heart that makes you speak so glibly?
UI: I speak the way I feel.
BETTY: Can anybody feel
  The way you speak? Perhaps he can. Your murders
  Come from the heart. Your blackest crimes are
  As deeply felt as other men's good deeds.
  As we believe in faith, so you believe in
  Betrayal. No good impulse can corrupt you.
  Unwavering in your inconstancy!

True to disloyalty, staunch in deception!
Kindled to sacred fire by bestial deeds!
The sight of blood delights you. Violence
Exalts your spirit. Sordid actions move you
To tears, and good ones leave you with deep-seated
Hatred and thirst for vengeance.

UI: Mrs Dullfeet
I always – it's a principle of mine –
Hear my opponent out, even when
His words are gall. I know that in your circle
I'm not exactly loved. My origins –
Never have I denied that I'm a humble
Son of the Bronx – are held against me.
'He doesn't even know,' they say, 'which fork
To eat his fish with. How then can he hope
To be accepted in big business? When
Tariffs are being discussed, or similar
Financial matters, he's perfectly capable
Of reaching for his knife instead of his pen.
Impossible! We can't use such a man!'
My uncouth tone, my manly way of calling
A spade a spade are used as marks against me.
These barriers of prejudice compel me
To bank exclusively on my own achievement.
You're in the cauliflower business. Mrs
Dullfeet, and so am I. There lies the bridge
Between us.

BETTY: And the chasm to be bridged
Is only foul murder.

UI: Bitter experience
Teaches me not to stress the human angle
But speak to you as a man of influence
Speaks to the owner of a greengoods business.
And so I ask you: How's the cauliflower
Business? For life goes on despite our sorrows.

BETTY: Yes, it goes on – and I shall use my life

To warn the people of this pestilence.
I swear to my dead husband that in future
I'll hate my voice if it should say 'Good morning'
Or 'Pass the bread' instead of one thing only:
'Extinguish Ui!'

GIRI, *in a threatening tone*: Don't overdo it, kid!

UI: Because amid the tombs I dare not hope
For milder feelings, I'd better stick to business
Which knows no dead.

BETTY: Oh Dullfeet, Dullfeet! Now
I truly know that you are dead.

UI: Exactly.
Bear well in mind that Dullfeet's dead. With him
Has died the only voice in Cicero
That would have spoken out in opposition
To crime and terror. You cannot deplore
His loss too deeply. Now you stand defenceless
In a cold world where, sad to say, the weak
Are always trampled. You've got only one
Protector left. That's me, Arturo Ui.

BETTY: And this to me, the widow of the man
You murdered! Monster! Oh, I knew you'd be here
Because you've always gone back to the scene of
Your crimes to throw the blame on others. 'No
It wasn't me, it was somebody else.'
'I know of nothing.' 'I've been injured'
Cries injury. And murder cries: 'A murder!
Murder must be avenged!'

UI: My plan stands fast.
Protection must be given to Cicero.

BETTY, *feebly*: You won't succeed.

UI: I will. That much I know.

BETTY: From this protector God protect us!

UI: Give
Me your answer.

He holds out his hand.

Is it friendship?

BETTY: Never while I live!
Cringing with horror, she runs out.
A sign appears.

14

Ui's bedroom at the Hotel Mammoth. Ui tossing in his bed, plagued by a nightmare. His bodyguards are sitting in chairs, their revolvers on their laps.

UI, *in his sleep*: Out, bloody shades! Have pity! Get you gone!
   The wall behind him becomes transparent. The ghost of Ernesto Roma appears, a bullet-hole in his forehead.
ROMA: It will avail you nothing. All this murder
   This butchery, these threats and slaverings
   Are all in vain, Arturo, for the root of
   Your crimes is rotten. They will never flower.
   Treason is made manure. Murder, lie
   Deceive the Clarks and slay the Dullfeets, but
   Stop at your own. Conspire against the world
   But spare your fellow conspirators.
   Trample the city with a hundred feet
   But trample not the feet, you treacherous dog!
   Cozen them all, but do not hope to cozen
   The man whose face you look at in the mirror!
   In striking me, you struck yourself, Arturo!
   I cast my lot with you when you were hardly
   More than a shadow on a bar-room floor.
   And now I languish in this drafty
   Eternity, while you sit down to table
   With sleek and proud directors. Treachery
   Made you, and treachery will unmake you.

Just as you betrayed Ernesto Roma, your
Friend and lieutenant, so you will betray
Everyone else, and all, Arturo, will
Betray you in the end. The green earth covers
Ernesto Roma, but not your faithless spirit
Which hovers over tombstones in the wind
Where all can see it, even the grave-diggers.
The day will come when all whom you struck down
And all you will strike down will rise, Arturo
And, bleeding but made strong by hate, take arms
Against you. You will look around for help
As I once looked. Then promise, threaten, plead.
No one will help. Who helped me in my need?

UI, *jumping up with a start*:
  Shoot! Kill him! Traitor! Get back to the dead!
  The bodyguards shoot at the spot on the wall indicated by Ui.

ROMA, *fading away*:
  What's left of me is not afraid of lead.

15

Financial District. Meeting of the Chicago vegetable dealers.
They are deathly pale.

FIRST VEGETABLE DEALER:
  Murder! Extortion! Highway robbery!

SECOND VEGETABLE DEALER:
  And worse: Submissiveness and cowardice!

THIRD VEGETABLE DEALER:
  What do you mean, submissiveness? In January
  When the first two came barging into
  My store and threatened me at gunpoint, I
  Gave them, a steely look from top to toe
  And answered firmly: I incline to force.

I made it plain that I could not approve
Their conduct or have anything to do
With them. My countenance was ice.
It said: So be it, take your cut. But only
Because you've got those guns.

FOURTH VEGETABLE DEALER: Exactly!
I wash my hands in innocence! That's what
I told my missus.

FIRST VEGETABLE DEALER, *vehemently*:
                    What do you mean, cowardice?
We used our heads. If we kept quiet, gritted
Our teeth and paid, we thought those bloody fiends
Would put their guns away. But did they? No! It's
Murder! Extortion! Highway robbery!

SECOND VEGETABLE DEALER:
Nobody else would swallow it. No backbone!

FIFTH VEGETABLE DEALER:
No tommy gun, you mean. I'm not a gangster.
My trade is selling greens.

THIRD VEGETABLE DEALER: My only hope
Is that the bastard some day runs across
Some guys who show their teeth. Just let him try his
Little game somewhere else!

FOURTH VEGETABLE DEALER: In Cicero
For instance.
The Cicero vegetable dealers come in. They are deathly pale.

THE CICERONIANS: Hi, Chicago!

THE CHICAGOANS: Hi, Cicero!
What brings *you* here?

THE CICERONIANS: We were told to come.

THE CHICAGOANS: By who?

THE CICERONIANS: By him.

FIRST CHICAGOAN: Who says so? How can he command
You? Throw his weight around in Cicero?

FIRST CICERONIAN: With
His gun.

SECOND CICERONIAN: Brute force. We're helpless.
FIRST CHICAGOAN: Stinking
   cowards!
  Can't you be men? Is there no law in Cicero?
FIRST CICERONIAN: No.
SECOND CICERONIAN: No longer.
THIRD CHICAGOAN: Listen, friends. You've got
   To fight. This plague will sweep the country
   If you don't stop it.
FIRST CHICAGOAN: First one city, then another.
   Fight to the death! You owe it to your country.
SECOND CICERONIAN:
   Why us? We wash our hands in innocence.
FOURTH CHICAGOAN:
   We only hope with God's help that the bastard
   Some day comes across some guys that show
   Their teeth.
   Fanfares. Enter Arturo Ui and Betty Dullfeet – in mourning –
   followed by Clark, Giri, Givola and bodyguards. Flanked by
   the others, Ui passes through. The bodyguards line up in the
   background.
GIRI: Hi, friends! Is everybody here
   From Cicero?
FIRST CICERONIAN: All present.
GIRI: And Chicago?
FIRST CHICAGOAN: All present.
GIRI, *to Ui*:   Everybody's here.
GIVOLA: Greetings, my friends. The Cauliflower Trust
   Wishes you all a hearty welcome. Our
   First speaker will be Mr Clark. *To Clark*: Mr Clark.
CLARK: Gentlemen, I bring news. Negotiations
   Begun some weeks ago and patiently
   Though sometimes stormily pursued – I'm telling
   Tales out of school – have yielded fruit. The wholesale
   House of I. Dullfeet, Cicero, has joined
   The Cauliflower Trust. In consequence

The Cauliflower Trust will now supply
Your greens. The gain for you is obvious:
Secure delivery. The new prices, slightly
Increased, have already been set. It is
With pleasure, Mrs Dullfeet, that the Trust
Welcomes you as its newest member.
Clark and Betty Dullfeet shake hands.

GIVOLA: And now: Arturo Ui.
Ui steps up to the microphone.

UI: Friends, countrymen!
Chicagoans and Ciceronians! When
A year ago old Dogsborough, God rest
His honest soul, with tearful eyes
Appealed to me to protect Chicago's green-
Goods trade, though moved, I doubted whether
My powers would be able to justify
His smiling confidence. Now Dogsborough
Is dead. He left a will which you're all free
To read. In simple words therein he calls me
His son. And thanks me fervently for all
I've done since I responded to his appeal.
Today the trade in vegetables –
Be they kohlrabi, onions, carrots or what
Have you – is amply protected in Chicago.
Thanks, I make bold to say, to resolute
Action on my part. When another civic
Leader, Ignatius Dullfeet, to my surprise
Approached me with the same request, this time
Concerning Cicero, I consented
To take that city under my protection.
But one condition I stipulated, namely:
The dealers had to want me. I would come
Only pursuant to their free decision
Freely arrived at. Cicero, I told
My men, in no uncertain terms, must not be
Subjected to coercion or constraint.

The city has to elect me in full freedom.
I want no grudging 'Why not?', no teeth-gnashing
'We might as well'. Half-hearted acquiescence
Is poison in my books. What I demand
Is one unanimous and joyful 'Yes'
Succinct and, men of Cicero, expressive.
And since I want this and everything else I want
To be complete, I turn again to you
Men of Chicago, who, because you know
Me better, hold me, I have reason to believe
In true esteem, and ask you: Who is for me?
And just in passing let me add: If anyone's
Not for me he's against me and has only
Himself to blame for anything that happens.
Now you may vote.

GIVOLA: But first a word from Mrs
Dullfeet, the widow, known to all of you, of
A man beloved by all.

BETTY: Dear friends
Your faithful friend and my beloved husband
Ignatius Dullfeet is no longer with us to . . .

GIVOLA: God rest his soul!

BETTY: . . . sustain and help you. I
Advise you all to put your trust in Mr
Ui, as I do now that in these grievous days
I've come to know him better.

GIVOLA: Time to vote!

GIRI: All those in favour of Arturo Ui
Raise your right hands!
Some raise their hands.

A CICERONIAN: Is it permissible to leave?

GIVOLA: Each man
Is free to do exactly as he pleases.
*Hesitantly the Ciceronian goes out. Two bodyguards follow him.
A shot is heard.*

GIRI: All right, friends, Let's have your free decision!
All raise both hands.

GIVOLA: They've finished voting, boss. With deep
    emotion
  Teeth chattering for joy, the greengoods dealers
  Of Cicero and Chicago thank you
  For your benevolent protection.

UI: With
  Pride I accept your thanks. Some fifteen years
  Ago, when I was only a humble, unemployed
  Son of the Bronx; when following the call
  Of destiny I sallied forth with only
  Seven staunch men to brave the Windy City
  I was inspired by an iron will
  To create peace in the vegetable trade.
  We were a handful then, who humbly but
  Fanatically strove for this ideal
  Of peace! Today we are a multitude.
  Peace in Chicago's vegetable trade
  Has ceased to be a dream. Today it is
  Unvarnished reality. And to secure
  This peace I have put in an order
  For more machine-guns, rubber truncheons
  Etcetera. For Chicago and Cicero
  Are not alone in clamouring for protection.
  There are other cities: Washington and Milwaukee!
  Detroit! Toledo! Pittsburgh! Cincinnati!
  And other towns where vegetables are traded!
  Philadelphia! Columbus! Charleston! And New York!
  They all demand protection! And no 'Phooey!'
  No 'That's not nice!' will stop Arturo Ui!
  Amid drums and fanfares the curtain falls.
  A sign appears.

Epilogue

Therefore learn how to see and not to gape.
To act instead of talking all day long.
The world was almost won by such an ape!
The nations put him where his kind belong.
But don't rejoice too soon at your escape –
The womb he crawled from still is going strong.

Chronological Table

1. 1929–1932. Germany is hard hit by the world crisis. At the height of the crisis a number of Prussian Junkers try to obtain government loans, for a long time without success. The big industrialists in the Ruhr dream of expansion.

2. By way of winning President Hindenburg's sympathy for their cause, the Junkers make him a present of a landed estate.

3. In the autumn of 1932, Adolf Hitler's party and private army are threatened with bankruptcy and disintegration. To save the situation Hitler tries desperately to have himself appointed Chancellor, but for a long time Hindenburg refuses to see him.

4. In January 1933 Hindenburg appoints Hitler Chancellor in return for a promise to prevent the exposure of the *Osthilfe* (East Aid) scandal, in which Hindenburg himself is implicated.

5. After coming to power legally, Hitler surprises his high patrons by extremely violent measures, but keeps his promises.

6. The gang leader quickly transforms himself into a statesman. He is believed to have taken lessons in declamation and bearing from one, Basil, a provincial actor.

7. February 1933, the Reichstag fire. Hitler accuses his enemies of instigating the fire and gives the signal for the Night of the Long Knives.

8. The Supreme Court in Leipzig condemns an unemployed worker to death for causing the fire. The real incendiaries get off scot-free.

9. and 10. The impending death of the aged Hindenburg provokes bitter struggles in the Nazi camp. The Junkers

and industrialists demand Röhm's removal. The occupation of Austria is planned.

11. On the night of 30 June 1934 Hitler overpowers his friend Röhm at an inn where Röhm has been waiting for him. Up to the last moment Röhm thinks that Hitler is coming to arrange for a joint strike against Hindenburg and Göring.

12. Under compulsion the Austrian Chancellor Engelbert Dollfuss agrees to stop the attacks on Hitler that have been appearing in the Austrian press.

13. Dollfuss is murdered at Hitler's instigation, but Hitler goes on negotiating with Austrian rightist circles.

15. On 11 March 1938 Hitler marches into Austria. An election under the Nazi terror results in a 98% vote for Hitler.

Notes

Page

6   *Givola steps back limping*: a direct reference to Goebbels'
disability – he had a club foot.
Since wars were fought for roses white and red?: the Wars of the
Roses, fought during the Middle Ages between the Houses of
Lancaster (red roses) and York (white), included Richard III's
violent seizure of the throne and concluded with his defeat by
Henry VII at the Battle of Bosworth in 1485.

7   Brecht wrote some additional lines to be inserted at the end of
the Prologue, evidently for a German audience after the end of
the Second World War:

> Ladies and gentlemen, the management's aware
> This is a controversial affair.
> Though some can still take history as they find it
> Most of you don't care to be reminded.
> Now, ladies and gentlemen, surely what this shows is
> Excrescences need proper diagnosis
> Conveyed not in some polysyllabic word
> But in plain speech that calls a turd a turd.
> Never mind if you're used to something more ethereal –
> The language of this play suits its material.
> Down from your gallows, then! Up from your graves!
> You murderous pack of filthy swindling knaves!
> Let's see you in the flesh again tonight
> And hope that in our present sorry plight
> Seeing the men from whom that plight first came
> Moves us not just to anger but to shame.

11   *Which one's soup do you prefer?*: whose charity handouts do you
     prefer to accept? The Salvation Army ran soup kitchens
     providing basic food for the unemployed and homeless.
     The ward boss on the waterfront: Dogsborough represents, on
     the local council, the people of the area containing the docks.
     Our old lunchroom operator: before Dogsborough went into
     local government, he ran the canteen, providing food for the
     workers at Sheet's docks. He now owns a restaurant.

14   *wilted shoes*: worn-out shoes so he looks poverty-stricken.

15   *won't save you from the hammer*: won't prevent you going
     bankrupt and having your property auctioned off to pay your
     creditors.

17   *Man doesn't live by bread/And meat alone, he needs his green
     goods*: humorous parody of Christian saying that 'Man does not
     live by bread alone', the assumption being that mankind needs
     spiritual as well as physical nourishment.

18   *the major share/Of stock in Sheet's shipyard*: as the largest
     shareholder he would in effect have control of the shipyard.

19   *it's not often that the gravy train/Travels the straight and
     narrow*: in business the 'gravy train' refers to the giving of such
     perks as free lunches to encourage business deals. It is not often
     that a society organised to fatten the financially unscrupulous
     chooses to adopt honest methods.

20   *there's no nigger in the woodpile*: a discredited racist saying
     which indicated something nasty lurking in the background,
     usually associated with a secret that those involved preferred to
     remain secret – probably originates from suspicion that black
     slaves stole firewood from their masters for their own use.

23–5 one of the three songs written for the Berliner Ensemble
     production was 'Ragg's Song':

          There was a little man
          He had a little plan
          They told him to go easy

> Just wait, my little man.
> But waiting made him queasy.
>> Heil Ui!
>> For he wants what he wants right now!
>>> (Derived from the 'Was-man-hat-hat-man Song' in scene 7 of
>>> *Round Heads and Pointed Heads*, GW *Stücke*, p. 993)

22   *in stir*: in prison.

24   *Posterity plaits no laurels for the gangster*: it was the custom in ancient Rome to crown victorious generals with wreaths of laurel leaves.

25   *Capone comes in/To buy some wreaths*: Al Capone, Chicago hoodlum, used to send wreaths to the funerals of those he had had 'eliminated'. Brecht parodies this in the later scene in Givola's flower shop.

29   *I've trodden the narrow path*: not strayed off the narrow path of good behaviour.

30   *the Bronx*: a rundown, poverty-stricken area of New York, emphasising Ui's poor origins. Ui uses this description of himself repeatedly.

32   *Down with the welshers!*: down with those who fail to repay their debts!

33   *I'll drill him*: shoot him so he's full of holes.

42   *Why not Abe Lincoln?*: Abraham Lincoln, President of the United States, was regarded as a by-word for honesty – emphasising the impossibility of believing that Dogsborough (Hindenburg) would be capable of such deception.

43   *a rod*: a gun.

47   *make/Him stop collecting hats*: one of Brecht's techniques for making sure the audience understand who has been the last to be killed by Giri, as well as underlining the gangster's disdain for his victims and for being suspected of murder.

47–8   by parodying Mark Antony's famous 'Friends, Romans, countrymen' speech in Shakespeare's *Julius Caesar*, Brecht draws attention to Ui's (Hitler's) inflated view of his own ambitions in relation to his actual abilities. The style of acting advocated by the actor and imitated by Ui represents one of the aspects of the German acting tradition which Brecht was determined should be abandoned.

50   *teamsters*: hauliers.

54   *One of the bodyguards steps forward and sings a sentimental song*: the song used in the Berliner Ensemble production was:

> A cabin stands beside the meadow
> It used to be my happy home.
> Now strangers' eyes are looking out the window
> Oh, why did I begin to roam?
> Home, take me home
> Back to my happy home!
> Home, take me home
> Back to my happy home!
> (Origin uncertain. Not Brecht.)

Fire on the waterfront!: on the quay or dockside.

62   *peculating*: embezzling.

63   at the end of the trial scene the Berliner Ensemble production inserted Givola's 'Whitewash Song':

> When the rot sets in, when walls and roof start dripping
> Something must be done at any price.
> Now the mortar's crumbling, bricks are slipping.
> If somebody comes it won't be nice.
> But whitewash will do it, fresh whitewash will do it.
> When the place caves in 'twill be too late.
> Give us whitewash, boys, then we'll go to it
> With our brushes till we fix things up first-rate.
> Now, here's a fresh disaster
> This damp patch on the plaster!
> That isn't nice. (No, not nice.)

Look, the chimney's falling!
Really, it's appalling!
Something must be done at any price.
Oh, if only things would look up!
This abominable fuck-up
Isn't nice. (No, not nice.)
But whitewash will do it, lots of white will do it.
When the place caves in 'twill be too late.
Give us whitewash, boys, then we'll go to it
And we'll whitewash till we've got it all first-rate.
Here's the whitewash, let's not get upset!
Day and night we've got the stuff on hand.
This old shack will be a palace yet.
You'll get your New Order, just as planned.

> (GW *Stücke* translated by Ralph Manheim, p. 936. This song
> originated as an appendage to Brecht's treatment ('The Bruise')
> for *The Threepenny Opera* film, and was then taken into *Round
> Heads and Pointed Heads*, where it is sung to a setting by Hanns
> Eisler as an interlude between scenes 2 and 3.)

67 *like blood spots*: recalls Brecht's description of the curtains for
staging *Arturo Ui*, that they should be spattered with blood.

69 *Are you boys trying to pressure me . . ./With nothing in my
naked/Hands but indomitable faith*: this speech demonstrates
Ui's command of the actor's training. His repetitions of 'faith'
provide the same irony as Mark Antony's use of 'honourable'
(see *Julius Caesar*, Act III, Scene II, lines 75–109).

72 *In ash and sackcloth*: another religious reference. In order to
demonstrate true repentance, sinners would dress in sackcloth
and smear their faces with ashes. Roma is contemptuous of
Dogsborough's guilt over his corrupt behaviour.
smells carrion: like a vulture hovering over rotting dead flesh,
Givola senses another victim.

73 *order handsome wreaths for Dogsborough./For Giri, too*: a

further reference to imitating Capone's custom of sending wreaths to his victims' funerals.

76–
80   A parody of the infamous St Valentine's Day Massacre when Al Capone eliminated a rival gang in a garage.

78   *Your hand/Is looking for its pole*: trembling like the arm of a compass before setting to point at the North Pole.

83–5   A parody of the scene in Goethe's *Faust* where Mephistopheles softens up Martha while Faust is preparing the ground for Gretchen's ruin.

88–
92   Parody of Shakespeare's *Richard III*, Act I, scene II, where Richard III woos Lady Anne over the coffin of her husband for whose murder Richard is responsible.

92–3   Parody of Shakespearean scenes where the ghosts of victims appear to haunt and taunt their murderers, for instance Banquo appearing to Macbeth.

96–7   In Ui's own version of 'Friends, Romans and countrymen!' Brecht underlines the rhetoric/reality gap, exposing the need for such a rise to be resisted.

98   *the Windy City*: a name for Chicago.
Some fifteen years/Ago . . . Unvarnished reality: parody of politicians' rhetoric, soaring to great heights and ending in the bathos of 'I have put in an order/For more machine-guns, rubber truncheons/Etcetera'.

98–9   The rising tide of exclamations in the last lines of Ui's final speech build to a climax, leaving Ui at the height of his powers. In the Berliner Ensemble production the Epilogue was spoken by Ekkehard Schall, stepping out of the persona of Ui. This directly demonstrates Brecht's intention of making the audience face his play's message: that the rise of such as Hitler must be resisted.

101   *Junkers*: East German landowners.
Reichstag: seat of government in Berlin.